THE CHANGING ROLE
OF RELIGIOUS LEADERS

The Once and Future Pastor

William Chris Hobgood

THE
ALBAN
INSTITUTE

Library of Congress Catalog Card #97-78130
ISBN 1-56699-200-1

CONTENTS

The issue is *leadership*—leadership anchored deep in faith. I am concerned about the emerging role of parish pastor. It has become clear that the behavior that summarizes the role most fully is *leadership*. The emerging church calls for a pastor who is well trained as a leader, assertive in leading, and faithful to God's mandate to be a servant leader.

As a judicatory minister I know that nothing in my work is more important than the health of the relationship between pastor and congregation. The pastor and the laity are in ministry together. But while I can help a congregation select a pastor, I cannot help it decide who will become members. While I have pastoral responsibility for the ministers, I can have little to do with whether members act constructively.

It had become clear to me that the future of the pastorate needed to be explored. Because we are at a turning point—due to the construction of the Gregorian calendar or owing to a real transition—this is the end of an era in congregational life.

It is more than a time when the calendar changes to a new century. It is a time to ask new questions about the next decades. Because of the ages of most American congregations, whether their members are young or older, an unprecedented transition faces us. Most congregations have moved beyond stability to a time of breakdown or crisis. Their futures are uncertain.

This book explores the changing roles of pastors at this transition point.

I approach this task from 37 years in ministry—25 in the pastorate and 13 in the middle judicatory. For much of this time I have trained, consulted, and conducted research about what makes pastorates work effectively. I chose to leave the pastorate to go into judicatory or "oversight ministry" because of a commitment to making pastorates healthier. I view my oversight responsibility as one of pastor to the relationship of pastor and congregation. Over the years, I have had one-on-one contacts with more than 400 congregations of varied sizes, communities, denominations, and ages.

But it is important to point out that this study is based on more than my own pastoral and oversight experience. Many of my colleagues likewise are experienced in pastorates and judicatories. To understand the issues more clearly, I designed a focused model for research. I conducted extended interviews with 32 ministers of what might be called "hot" congregations. These congregations are growing in more than one facet of church life: stewardship, evangelism, spirituality, and compassion. I will describe these modes of growth in detail in chapter four. For the moment, it is important to note that growth does not mean mindless numerical expansion.

These interviews were conducted in person, by telephone, or in small focus groups. All pastors responded to the same interview sequence, including information about the pastor's background, tenure in the present pastorate, and other general data. A four-faceted growth model was posed to them, and they were asked to look at their ministry in the present congregation through this lens. Then they were asked to assess relationship(s) in their pastorates from the standpoint of trust, and to describe their leadership styles. Responses to these questions are presented in chapter five in a descriptive narrative about leadership that forms the core of that chapter.

Finally, each pastor was asked to react to four leadership styles. The four suggested styles were "telling," "selling," "facilitating," and "collaborating." This model, which I designed, is based on my experience with a variety of approaches to leadership styles. My premise is that the most effective leader can function in any of these styles when appropriate but will value and use some styles more than others.

The 32 pastors interviewed came from a range of places and from several theological perspectives. They represented eight denominations. Eight of the pastors are women. Ten are African American, one is Asian American, 21 are European American. Their average time in ministry since ordination is 21.4 years, and the average tenure in their present pastorates is 14.3 years. The women interviewed had an average tenure of 8.4 years, and the men 16.5 years. It is notable that these pastors' tenures are significantly longer than the average pastorate—about seven years. This makes relevant a question about the relation of tenure to productivity in a pastor's leadership.

These subjects were not chosen randomly. Rather, I sought pastors of congregations that had demonstrated, during this pastor's tenure, at least two expressions of growth based on the four-dimensional growth model described in chapter four. I was also interested in selecting congregations that were evenly distributed across the congregational life cycle (chapter four). More were chosen from my own denomination, the Christian Church (Disciples of Christ), than from any other, only because of my deep knowledge and numerous contacts there. Names came from various sources, including Leadership Network and colleagues in the Alban Institute and various ecumenical and community groups.

This sample is not intended to be statistically accurate. Rather, the idea was to identify a solid group of growing-edge congregations and discern what is happening in them. From them, I believe, we can all learn for tomorrow.

Several of the congregations could be called "niche" churches, a type described in chapter one. Niche congregations examined here include one that appeals uniquely to gay and lesbian people, another whose mission is political activism in the nation's capital, and a church with a particular call to people involved with the arts. Most, however, including these three, would extend a warm welcome to all.

I want to acknowledge and thank the 32 pastors. They are practitioners of faithful, creative, and often courageous pastoral ministry. I am grateful that they have allowed us a look into their ministries so that we can learn for ours. Their names follow.

The Rev. Anne Bonney, Brookhaven Christian Church, Atlanta, Ga.
The Rev. David Caldwell, First Christian Church, Baltimore, Md.
The Rev. William Calhoun, Trinity Baptist Church, Baltimore, Md.
The Rev. Delores Carpenter, Michigan Park Christian Church, Washington, D.C.
The Rev. George Claddis, Covenant Presbyterian Church, Austin, Tex.
The Rev. Vernon Dobson, Union Baptist Church, Baltimore, Md.
The Rev. Marshall Dunn, University Christian Church, Hyattsville, Md.
The Rev. Graylon Ellis-Hagler, Plymouth United Church of Christ, Washington, D.C.

The Rev. David Emery, Woodlands Christian Church, The Woodlands, Tex.

The Rev. Laurinda Hafner, Pilgrim United Church of Christ, Cleveland, Ohio

The Rev. Cynthia Hale, Ray of Hope Christian Church, Atlanta, Ga.

The Rev. H. Beecher Hicks, Metropolitan Baptist Church, Washington, D.C.

The Rev. Alvin O. Jackson, Mississippi Boulevard Christian Church, Memphis, Tenn.

The Rev. Roger Kim, Grace Life Church, Baltimore, Md.

The Rev. Kathleen Kline-Chesson, Henson Valley Christian Church, Fort Washington, Md.

The Rev. Janet Long, Washington Ave. Christian Church, Elyria, Ohio

The Rev. Kyle Maxwell, First Christian Church, Edmond, Okla.

The Rev. Jack Morris, Largo Community Church, Largo, Md.

The Rev. Fred McCormick, executive for program, Wooddale Church, Eden Prairie, Minn.

The Rev. Larry Osborne, North Coast Church, Vista, Calif.

The Rev. John O. Peterson, Alfred Street Baptist Church, Alexandria, Va.

The Rev. Gary Pinder, Lewinsville Presbyterian Church, McLean, Va.

The Rev. Joan Robey, Findley Street Christian Church, Seattle, Wash.

The Rev. Charles Shields, Brentwood Presbyterian Church, Brentwood, Calif.

The Rev. Ernest Smart, Second Presbyterian Church, Baltimore, Md.

The Rev. Lonnie Southern, Fairfax Christian Church, Fairfax, Va.

The Rev. Timothy Spears, Dickeyville Presbyterian Church, Dickeyville, Md.

The Rev. Randall Spleth, Geist Christian Church, Indianapolis, Ind.

The Rev. A. Knighton Stanley, Peoples' Congregational United Church of Christ, Washington, D.C.

The Rev. Gary Straub, First Christian Church, Frankfort, Ky.

The Rev. Joanne Verberg, Covenant Christian Church, Carey, N.C.

The Rev. Joaquin Willis, Amistad United Church of Christ, Landover, Md.

I wish I could also name the hundreds of other colleagues whose ministries have provided fodder for my thinking for years. To those men and women, may I simply ask, if you read this book, to consider this word my thanks for your colleagueship and the openness of your ministry to deeper understanding.

I am grateful to Loren Mead, whose rich mind and hearty love of the church have pushed many of us to stretch in unforeseen directions. I thank the staff of the Christian Church-Capital Area for their generosity in giving me time to work on this, and I thank my wife, Cary Meade, who has put up with a lot over the years because of my vocation and interests—most recently the time and space taken to do this project. She is an amazing friend and supporter.

CHAPTER 1

Ministry at the Crossroads

The young pastor took me to lunch, a final visit before he left the secure associate minister position he had held for two years to move into his first solo parish pastorate. He brimmed with both excitement and anxiety. After lunch and light talk he asked me the question that had prompted him to call me. "You have been in this business for a long time. You seem to know your way around. Please tell me: what is the single most important thing you would like me to remember as I go into this new life?"

After a flip reply and then a serious conversation, I began a process of thinking that led to a study and to this book. There *is* no single most important matter. The reality is that as ministers face tomorrow there may be almost too much to remember, for pastoral ministry has become immensely more complex than ever before.

Let's look at two examples from different eras. My uncle Thomas, who retired more than 40 years ago, gave 50 years to being a pastor— one of Kentucky's finest, and a prominent citizen as well. His pastoral ministry emphasized community visibility, visits with sick and shut-in parishioners, committee meetings to plan more of the good work already being done, construction of church buildings, leadership of worship and the shaping of stirring sermons, and the important functions of performing marriages and funerals and representing the church in the community's life.

Much later, my daughter Laura was associate minister of a large congregation in the Midwest. There she led a team of lay leaders in developing a comprehensive program of youth activities, including outreach, a traveling choral program, and counseling for troubled young people. In addition, she was staff resource to two congregational planning teams, co-worship planner and leader, and participant in a host of concerns about the future of the congregation's teaching and community ministries. She also gave special attention to young adults both single and married, being the one person on staff who could relate believably to people just finding their way back to the church.

It is clear that if we want to understand the life of the church as it moves into a new century, we must look at the clergy, tomorrow's shepherds. The demands on Thomas and Laura were different, and the demands on most pastors today become increasingly complicated. What will be asked of them in this extraordinary time?

The basis for this exploration is not the fact of a turning century or millennium, but a church overtaken by social, cultural, technological, ecological, and theological forces that are upending pillars upon which the church has stood for decades, even centuries. That a crisis faces us at a time when the calendar turns to a new century is a matter more of coincidence than of divine intervention. But because we face this turning time, it is vital to pose some questions about tomorrow's shepherds. What will they be like? What *should* they try to be? Should the church revise its ways of preparing pastors for tomorrow?

Two Pastors

It is as though, for a brief moment, God has given us time to try to understand pastoral ministry at this remarkable crossroads. Consider two pastors.

He has been minister of First Church for ten years. Most of that time has been filled with excitement, change, and varying degrees of turbulence. She is the first woman called to be pastor of St. Mark's. It has not been easy.

- "His preaching is becoming more personal every week. He just seems angry at all of us."

- "She doesn't appear to have the gentle patience she came with. She has changed."

- "He is the most skilled minister I have ever known, and in this parish he needs all of it and then some. We place incredible demands on him."

- "She is always thoroughly prepared, whether it is for worship, preaching, or meetings. Why, she even seems ready for casual conversations. How can she possibly have time or energy for all of this? She must really get tired."

- "We are a very diverse congregation, with people of several racial groups as well as different beliefs about the faith. Our pastor works very hard at encouraging these differences. We don't always agree, but somehow he keeps bringing new and different people in. I hope it doesn't drive the old-timers out."

- "Pastor Ruth really does relate well to younger families. It's not only because she and Jim have small kids themselves, but she really attracts them. Of course, some of the older folks think she spends all her time with the newer ones."

- "Ed has brought a lot of change to our church in the ten years since he became pastor. We needed a lot of it. But I'm not so sure about some of the things we do in worship. What will we do next?"

- "She has a way of loving us *and* pushing us at the same time. We love her love for us. We don't always love her pushing."

This random selection of comments could apply to many parish ministers who seek to fulfill the high vocation to which God has called them.

There was a time not long ago when life for parish clergy was far simpler and more predictable, and they received enough respect and support from members and the wider community to boost their spirits in both good and difficult moments. But this state of affairs is changing. The clergy have changed, as the world and religious communities have changed. More than 40 percent of clergy who graduate from seminary are women, a percentage expected to continue growing. For nearly two decades a growing number of students have come to seminary after first careers, bringing to their training for ministry far different life experiences from those of the young student straight out of college. Diversity of gender, ethnic constituencies, theological beliefs, varied gifts for ministry, and more typically urban than rural backgrounds—these qualities describe the emerging pastoral ministry.

Today's world, called by some "post-religious," is market-driven, consumer-conscious, celebrity-fixated, politically polarized, and dividing rapidly into two populations—a small village of people with great wealth and a very large city of the poor. This world often seems to have moved as far from faith in God as possible while still retaining some degree of sanity. The religious world is struggling, in Loren Mead's image, to find the new paradigm, the third great stage of meaning and focus, while the "Christendom" paradigm, in which "the world is the mission field," breaks down.[1] Congregations, led by their pastors, must be in the front lines of the search for this new paradigm. We don't know everything about this new pattern, but we are beginning to discern some of its crucial parts, and it is to the pastor's role in this process that this book is committed.

We stand at a crossroads, moving at a pace so rapid that tomorrow comes before we are ready. Traditional words and ways are inadequate to tell the wonderful old story in this new world, and we hear ourselves mumble as we struggle to find fresh phrases. The great, gracious, committed but sometimes stubborn and stodgy saints who have borne the church's loads for the past 50 years are aging, retiring, dying. They leave in their place new generations, some of whose members are seekers with fresh expectations, rich skills, impatience, little time for traditional church work, a disinclination to be the kinds of stewards on which the church still depends, a spirituality that may seem frighteningly personal, and a worldliness that appears almost brazen in its taunting of tradition.

What will happen, at this complex crossroads, to the familiar institutions of faith? To delve into this conundrum, let's look at pastoral ministry from the perspectives of four parishes, each stuck in a different rut.

Four Congregations

Growing, But Only in One Way

Holy Name Church in Centerville got off to a fast start in coping with
the new times members found themselves entering. Nearly two decades
ago, Holy Name began seeing community change coming. Members saw
a second great migration heading their way. Two decades earlier, the
neighboring big city had begun to stretch its boundaries. Around Centerville—a small town a few miles from the city—farmers began yielding
land to developers. Cornfields were replaced by cul-de-sacs. Farmhouses
were out; ranch houses were in. The deliberate pace of Centerville, its
settled middle-of-the-road routine, disappeared as quickly as the seasons,
and just as suddenly the Centre Mall appeared.

For Holy Name this boom in construction seemed a windfall. Pastor
James was a brilliant strategist and marketer, and with the support of
several key lay leaders, members began a program of recruitment that
resulted in hundreds of new members each year. With laity schooled in
what they called "invitational evangelism," dozens of new visitors appeared nearly every week. Each was visited within 24 hours, often for
only a few moments, the callers bringing cookies or some other sign of
welcome. In two weeks, if the newcomer returned to worship or church
school, he or she was visited again, this time by a team of people who
had much in common with the individual. In another two weeks the pastor visited, most of the time inviting the newcomer to join, and even
setting the date for reception into membership.

Holy Name's program was the talk of the town, the area, the state,
the denomination. No other mainline church could compare. From 200
members to 2,000 in just seven years!

But Holy Name had a problem. The traditional offerings of worship
and church school, youth groups and women's circles, bazaars and co-
vered-dish dinners didn't hold these new people. Many drifted away.
Holy Name had done a marvelous job of personal recruitment and evangelism. But the assumption that business-as-usual inside the doors would
hold these newcomers was problematic. The congregation really hadn't
thought of changing its interior life to accommodate a massive influx of
new friends and members. The parish did genuinely welcome newcomers,
and members' warmth was palpable. But there were more satisfying

activities for the newcomers elsewhere. Without having planned it that
way, Holy Name became a revolving door.

To Survive Is to Die

Faith Church, Jackson, "was a really good church at one time," the
people said. This statement became their mantra, as they sadly reached
for ways to recover the past. In time, only memories remained to give
them a reason to live.

Faith Church had been founded by people who left a failing urban
congregation. For years they had tried, but nothing had worked as their
city changed. So they left and bought land in a growing part of the city,
only to realize that they were within two miles of two other congregations of their denomination—the kind of insight that, strangely, often
comes too late.

Faith Church was rescued by a group of doctors who offered them
far more money for their land than they had paid for it. With this second
chance, the faithful band looked to a far edge of town, where rapid
growth was taking place. There they settled, able now to afford twice
the acreage and a spacious, functional, attractive new building.

For a few years the parish thrived.Young families, always the most
desired objects of mainline congregations' evangelism, came in good
numbers. Programs were organized for this influx. An associate minister
concentrated on children and youth ministries. A community recreation
center for youth attracted new people. Because the congregation was
near a large high school, partnership in the neighborhood was the norm.

But another urban shift spelled trouble for Faith Church. The middle-
class, white, upwardly mobile residents were moving to neighborhoods
ten miles away. Within a few years the neighborhood where Faith
Church had prospered became a multiracial, lower-middle-class, crime-
infested urban dilemma.

Faith Church, whose lifestyle had been attuned to a certain pattern
of growth, found matters moving beyond its reach. The members hunk-
ered down. Staying alive became the primary goal. But staying alive
came to mean just keeping the doors open, paying the bills, and holding
worship services. The pastor of many years seemed equally depressed.
Like a hiker whose boots get mired in a bog, the more they reached
back for the past, the deeper they found themselves stuck.

Finally, it seemed, members made an unconscious decision not to try anymore, and to mark time until something happened, whatever that might be.

Where There Is Low Soul

Old Queensboro Church, unlike most churches in the community, did not have a long history. The other congregations in town averaged 225 years of age. Old Q, as members fondly called it, was only 65. That the town was preoccupied with its history may have been one of Old Q's problems. Not old enough to have gained the awed respect of the city's ruling fathers and mothers, yet no longer an infant, Old Q found itself in a hard spot.

This congregation had quickly gone through periods of founding, growth, and strong vitality; now it struggled with the future. Some members could recall the days of formation, the beloved first pastor, other early leaders, and vital parts of Old Q's story. Several had lived through the times of expansion and power; their memories held images of crowded rooms and enthusiastic volunteers, generous offerings and hearty youth groups. Memory and myth were blended. Those were the days!

The young pastor had in five years led the members through a time of renewal and re-visioning. All the right processes were followed, a fresh vision was put into words, and everything seemed to be in place for a new era of congregational growth. Why not? After all, this place had good people, enough strong stewards to afford the minimum budget, talented leaders—why should it not grow again?

But a dark cloud hung over Old Q. The congregation went through the motions. With a strong choir, youth activities that still attracted new kids, and a relatively healthy stewardship program, everything seemed right.

And yet no one could grab hold of the new vision with any zeal. It was all right so long as the focus stayed on things in the here and now. But mentioning the future sent people running for cover. No one wanted to talk about tomorrow. It was as though the members simply didn't believe there would be a tomorrow. After all, what could surpass the days of flourishing?

An elephant-like pace prevailed in much of Old Q's life. Bogged down: that was the descriptive term. Like a person suffering severe depression, members nixed whatever idea was suggested. No one thought anything new would go right. People quit wondering if the Holy Spirit was present. They lost zeal, hope, confidence, and will. It seemed only a matter of time for Old Q. Although they have different histories, Faith and Old Q have arrived at similar destinations.

Everything To Everyone

St. John's Church is a strong congregation in many traditionally acceptable ways. Begun nearly 50 years ago as a result of a congregational split over a conflict about a pastor, St. John's appeared successful early in its life, contrary to the norm of churches with such beginnings. Numbers increased, good stewards and stewardship programs grew, and the congregation developed a well-rounded program to meet the parish's needs. Members built a fine building, gave strong financial and volunteer support to community and larger church efforts, and developed a strong organization. Many skilled lay leaders came forward, including large numbers experienced in government-related organizations. For most it seemed a dream congregation, with a strong program and support, good lay leaders, and active members of all generations. Everything seemed fine—at least for the first two decades.

Then the effects of change began to appear. The average age of St. John's members increased steadily. Today more than half of the members are 65 or over. A few of their children stayed, and some came back after extended absences. There are middle-aged members, but not many. Some younger families and singles have joined in recent years, and while they bring energy to St. John's, they also bring needs and wants that stretch this congregation's capacities, for St. John's has never stopped trying to be everything to everyone.

It is not a "niche" congregation—that is, one that serves a particular cultural or theological constituency.[2] It does not serve just one neighborhood. Indeed, the neighborhood's predominant ethnicity has changed three times during St. John's 50 years. St. John's has lived on because people come from far and near. With a varied membership, St. John's, even today, tries to do everything it can for everyone.

The congregation now has some problems with this approach. For one thing, there are fewer than half as many volunteers for day-to-day tasks as before, since former volunteers are either too old or employed full time, and today's economics require that just about all younger adults work. Those laypeople who still serve willingly tend to hold leadership roles, still exerting mighty powers, sometimes in conflict with clergy leaders over who is in charge, presiding over programs and priorities that look eerily like those of three decades ago.

A sense of immobilization charactizes efforts in new directions. The older members feel that things are fine, thank you. Middle-aged and younger members sometimes disagree, but those who object vociferously are soon hushed by the sheer will and strength of the older lay leaders, and they either leave or give in. St. John's is headed for burnout and doesn't know it.

And So . . .

These represent four examples of congregations at the crossroads. Each demonstrates an acute dilemma of congregational life. Each seems stuck in that dilemma. None stands ready to move with new vitality.

Any person who cares about a congregation and congregational life would do well to reflect on whether his or her congregation is visible in any of these pictures. Even more important, what is the congregation's view of ministry, particularly of pastoral ministry?

For the foreseeable future, the pastor's leadership will be pivotal for the congregation's vitality and renewal. As we shall see, congregations emerging as vital centers of mission and ministry are those whose pastors give significant leadership. To do so, they must accommodate the many ways in which their roles are changing. Coming chapters will identify and explain those changes.

CHAPTER 2

Tomorrow's Promise

But we are not of those who shrink back and so are lost, but among those who have faith and so are saved. Now faith is the assurance of things hoped for, the conviction of things not seen.

(Heb. 10:39, 11:1)

What a heroic declaration! This statement about faith is grounded in faith. Otherwise, how could it be spoken?

Such a faith *does* seem easier said than done, even in the church, a body formed in and focused on faith. Powerful forces cause us to shrink back from the future. We face tomorrow with both hope and hesitation. Doubt, despair, caution, and fear all hinder our faithfulness to the call to a faith focused on the future. Forces that bind the church and hinder its growth in this bold faith say such things as "We have to preserve what we've got," or "We cannot do anything foolish," or "Let's take it easy," or "This isn't the right time to do that."

The utter naivete with which the author of Hebrews would have us strike forth in daring faith seems foolhardy to some of the seasoned. This fresh challenge to move threatens the stability and viability of an institution cherished, just *because* it has stayed the same. After all, everything else is changing. Isn't it right that the church be the one institution on which people can rely for steadiness and constancy?

Based on such thinking, we often enact some very potent deeds. For example, we maintain an ethnic "sameness" of membership, or of economic class, theological persuasion, or even age, in our congregations, thus minimizing conflict and resulting change. Also, we are often cold toward trying new programs, for these could engage new people in the congregation. Such actions as these prevent the church's movement.

Deeply rooted in fear, the church's resistance constitutes a mighty force. Each mode of resistance offers a lens through which we can view the effect of the future on church people today. As mirrors for the clergy, what do they tell us about the ways pastors view the future and act as a new century draws near?

Faith and Future Shock

Nearly three decades ago Alvin Toffler introduced the term "future shock" to our contemporary vocabulary. Future shock is "the dizzying disorientation brought on by the premature arrival of the future."[1] Note the difference between the common image that we are moving toward tomorrow and the uncommon one (Toffler's) that tomorrow is moving toward us. It is as though we are sitting in a theater while sophisticated technologies create the sensation that tomorrow is rushing headlong toward us.

Events since Toffler's book bear him out. He wrote hard on the heels of what religious sociologists Wade Clark Roof and William McKinney have called "an almost artificial prosperity" for the religious world of the 50s in America.[2] The turbulent 60s disrupted that age of plenty for churches, but the 50s were still recent enough for many to believe the glory days could be recaptured.

When Toffler wrote about future shock, the communications revolution was still only a dream to some bold engineers. Miniaturization, the process that has made computers household items, hadn't become common knowledge. I recall a mid-60s tour of the NASA facility at Greenbelt, Maryland, where, in an example of the day's most sophisticated technology, a large room with great banks of ceiling-high computers maintained contact with the most recent artificial space-based satellites. Today the capabilities of those ten massive crates of wires and fuses can be contained in the "brain" of one three-pound laptop computer. The world today is highly dependent on such technology.

Similarly, the religious world is being affected by future shock in ways we still don't comprehend. Until ten years ago, cycles of congregational life could be expected to last about seven years. A cycle is a period in which the congregation has one primary area of emphasis, such as community mission, stewardship, nurture, or any other area critical to the congregation's life. Seven years was a normal timespan for which to plan and act. By the end of seven years the constituency, community, and consensus would change enough to call for a new focus, and it would be important to move to a new area of emphasis, while seeking to retain gains from that seven-year focus.

Today a congregation dare not plan a ministry emphasis lasting more than three years. Membership, community needs, technologies, stewardship resources, information, biblical scholarship—all have a shorter shelf life.

The shelf life of computer software is a metaphor that fits much in these times. Replacement time is shorter. To some degree, the software industry creates this need to replace things quickly, by a variation of what Vance Packard decades ago called "planned obsolescence," in which products are designed to wear out and need replacement within a limited time. In the case of current computer products, the pace of invention and improvement is so rapid that products may be obsolete before we plug them in. Discovery in technology has an explosive character. It leaps forward, not always knowing where it will go. New worlds are being created at incredible speed.

Notable Changes in Organized Religion

Forces acting unpredictably on organized religion these days demonstrate our difficulty with future shock. Three are most notable: changes in the membership of religious institutions, different ways of financing the church, and diminishing esteem for religious institutions.

Changes in membership

Numbers of congregations these days speak of "how old we are." They don't mean their corporate age but the average age of members. Despite important exceptions, most congregations are small, built around one or two dominant families. The bulk of core members are aging, and they are not being replaced by younger people. Many young people whose parents are of the postwar Baby Boom generation chose to leave the church.

Some are returning, but massive numbers are thoroughly secularized and apparently have no intention of returning. This trend makes the future shaky for many congregations, because a membership whose average age is 65-plus does not guarantee permanence. Even as congregations try to understand this problem, Generation X, born from 1965 to 1983, and the subsequent cohort are already on the scene. Will they stay or come back? We do not know.

Changes in Finances

This same reality has a dramatic effect on church finances. The post-World War II generation provided the financial support for American religious institutions for four decades. Now its members are aging and dying. Their children are either absent or less schooled in dedicated stewardship. Religious organizations have begun to seek out new ways to fund their lives. These funding mechanisms are not as simple as pledges and tithes, weekly commitments, and giving out of a trust in the institution to which one gives. (See *"Plain Talk About Churches and Money,"* by Dean Hoge, et al. [the Alban Institute, 1997][3] for a detailed discussion of this reality.)

Diminished Esteem for the Church

The world doesn't pay much attention to organized faith groups these days, particularly more traditional ones. One of the biggest religious stories of 1997 in the United States was the Washington, D.C., Mall rally of the "Promise Keepers"—a religious story to be sure, but not one related to any historic, established religious body. Indeed, such groups deliberately shun identifying with an existing religious body, as though to do so would poison their appeal. Public-policy lobbying by religious groups may evoke such responses from congressional staffers as, "We don't see any religious representatives anymore," and "Do people really pay much attention to what the churches are saying?" At one time the Southern Baptist Convention boycotted Disney products for reasons of principle. Some thought this action might even increase Disney's appeal to consumers.

The future is coming toward us rapidly. How do we respond to to-morrow when tomorrow is already here and we feel that we must spend ourselves bracing for its next onslaught?

The Call of the Status Quo: Backing into Tomorrow

Faced with all of this disorienting change, isn't it tempting to hang on and preserve those wonderful gains we've made over the years? "Status quo" means "the existing state of affairs."[4] To maintain the status quo means to hang on to what is. Change is hard work. It requires adapting to new circumstances. Putting on a new garment always means shucking old stuff. If you want to wear two suits, don't pretend that it is comforta-ble or that your mobility is unimpaired in that stifling garb.

The church cannot wear two suits.Yet we try. We seek to reach a new age with the always-new Word, but the methods of reaching are often as outdated as is communicating by beating drums amid banks of telephones and Internet-wired computers.

Extensive inquiry has identified three areas where this difficulty is most obvious: worship, mission, and structure.

Worship, a Changing Place

The current struggle in many traditional congregations is whether to have "alternative worship." Should we offer opportunities for people to engage the Holy with contemporary music, personal testimonies, less formal dress, spontaneous praise and prayer? Or do we see this style as a passing phase, and choose to keep the same hymns, prayers, rituals, and sermon styles that our parents treasured? When many come to the church for sanctuary from the turbulence of the world and their personal communities, change in worship—the most cherished part of the church's life—can be terribly disorienting. For many worshipers, the goal is peaceful satisfaction, not energizing stimulation. Many of those who want things to stay the same are intelligent, driven, high-energy people. They want the church to be the one place where they are not continually pushed to consider new possibilities. It is an anchor in the storm.

At the same time, the manners and practices of worship are under fire today. Why? Because two generations have been turned off by traditional religion and its rituals. People under 50 are products of media messages, shaped by "instant" everything from coffee to computers, who can tune in at home to the latest movies and offer their word to the world by using the World Wide Web. These people are not looking for a 1910 worship experience. From second-generation Koreans in the United States who reject their immigrant parents' desire to worship in Korean, to the Promise Keepers, who flock to stadiums and the Washington Mall for nondenominational rallies of prayer, community, and recommitment, most members of new-style religious communities are young and attracted to new forms of celebration.

But it is not simple to make this concession—and it *is* viewed by many traditionalists as a concession. To concede seems to say, "I was wrong." Crow does not taste good, however you cook it. Worship is one scene where the status quo calls loudly and clearly to many.

Mission at Our Doorsteps

The fundamental question in mission practice is one of trust. For decades mission appeared to be going well. American or European Missionary societies that sent any applicant who wanted to go and was fit for the work have now given way to partnerships in which young Christians of the Third World are seen to be as competent as the mission boards to make decisions about their lives. Traditional missionary activity seemed to presume that the missionary was culturally superior to the person being served. The new mission trusts the recipient to shape his or her own values and practices. Whether this scenario is played out in Africa or Arizona, God's will is not well served when we fail to trust one another, particularly in locales where people risk their health and lives to serve our Saviour. Yet many congregations and denominations still assume a form of mission in which they "go to" rather than "serve with" others. The change from missionary church to servant church is a difficult transition. But it is necessary at a time when the church's mission begins at its own doorstep.

Structures: Will They Adapt?

A third pressure point in the church is structure. Not long after the end
of World War II, denominations discovered structures that would include as many people as possible on the committees that shaped the
congregation's life. This inclusion had two good effects: it took control
from the hands of a few older men, and it brought a cross-section of each
congregation's membership into planning, deciding, and therefore own-
ing the church's life. Oddly enough, the start of this basically inclusive
institutional transformation preceded the gender-equality movement by
20 years.

Yet this change resulted, in time, in congregations spending more
time trying to fill committee rosters than in doing the committee's work.
In effect, the tail spent a lot of time wagging the dog, as satisfying the
organizational pattern became the church's driving force. In many congregations it became a rule that structure must be followed. The reality,
many are discovering, is that inflexible structures do not lend themselves to creative life.

And so we move on, adhering to status quo, somehow believing that
we can best meet (or avoid) the future by backing into it. Whether locked
in an inflexible structure, absorbed by nostalgia, immobilized by fear of
the new, or bound by rejection of anyone with a different idea, we spend
our time resisting forward movement and the exciting work of finding
new ways to proclaim God's ancient truth.

Like It or Not, Congregations Change

A grudging acknowledgment that change is real can subtly lead to a
last line of resistance to change's demands. We say "Yes, I guess so" to
change, and then we add, with emphasis, "*But!*" Do we view change as
enemy or friend? As a welcome process or as something to be accepted
reluctantly?

Churches can be as energetic about holding change at bay, even as
they admit its presence. Listen to a case in point. A well-known urban
congregation in a great city called a new pastor. The "flagship" congregation of its denomination, this church struggled for three years to find
the right pastor. The church had had a long pastorate, 19 years, during
which finances, community ministries, and strong linkages with other

parts of the denomination had all grown. The retiring pastor was loved by many. How could anyone succeed such a great servant? Finally, after two abortive attempts, a pastor was called. He was the best-known rising minister of the denomination. A great preacher, he had also led a former congregation to a 3,000 percent growth in membership and finances. A man of deep faith and spirituality, he said yes because he heard God calling him to this new ministry. The call was unique, for the congregation is historically Euro-American, and the newly called pastor is African-American. Except for a handful of questioners, the vote to call was strong and enthusiastic.

Just about everyone owned up to the truth that change was on its way. But in the wings there lurked some anxieties, including whispered yearnings:

- "Let's not become an all-black congregation."
- "Will gays and lesbians still be welcomed here?"
- "If we grow in numbers, do we really have to become huge?"

So change was secretly an enemy to some, though the vote to call was strong. Change is a reality, but isn't there still time to contain it, manage it, shape it, and form it in ways that are not radical outgrowths of who and what we are now?

Three Ways to Change

There are three ways to plan for tomorrow. I call them reaction, perpetuation, and anticipation. The first two, used alone, are essentially ways of guaranteeing that, while we make concessions to change, as much of today as possible is preserved. In these cases, the energy that propels change is *not* the call of tomorrow but the contentment offered by today. A brief examination of these two ways will help us understand how much they allow us to control our responses to change.

Change by Reaction

A reactive way to approach the future says that we prepare for tomorrow by simply responding to the needs that we see today. Without question, people of faith need to respond to needs as they discern them. When the media tell us that millions of children are starving in the Sahel, we have no choice but to act. When a whole race is denied its most basic humanity because laws are immoral and one-sided, as in South Africa's apartheid years, then we do what must be done to ensure that justice rules. When one of every four children is born into poverty in the United States, the economic system must be radically changed. When the kids in the church have no program, not even a good nursery during worship, then we either meet their needs or lose their families to the church.

Reacting and responding to felt needs is an important part of how we look at today. But if it is the only way we plan, with no thought given to the future, then we will ignore the larger reality of change, the tides and currents, the signs of coming storms, and all the other ways in which we discern what God is calling us to do and to be tomorrow. Furthermore, if we plan only by reacting, then much will be done not in response to genuine need but in response to constituencies that have learned to make the case that their need is greatest.

Change by Perpetuation

A style of perpetuation seems at first bolder, more deliberate, with far more initiative toward tomorrow. It is more proactive than reactive. To use perpetuation is to move out, not listening to needs and interests.

The perpetuation method describes the person or group that simply continues boldly and enthusiastically to do more of what has been done all along, whether it is needed or not, and even if no one comes. To paraphrase an old peace poster, "Suppose they held a church bazaar and no one came?" The perpetuative group will keep on holding bazaars regardless. This mode works from a stance of "what we want and have to offer" rather than "what the world needs of us."

Religious institutions are not, historically and culturally, organizations from which change is most readily expected. After all, do we not base our very being on the reality of a God who, from our perspective, is changeless? Even process theology, which speaks of God being still in process and growing, affirms that such God-graces as love and patience only grow, remaining unchanging in their fundamental character.

So we resist change. But the resistance is often less denial than it is a grudging acceptance and a desire that change come to us only on our terms. While confessing that change comes, we want to control it. Giving it a brief nod, we go on with our agendas.

Anticipating Change: Where Is God Calling Us?

"*Is* God calling us?" may be the prior question. From a theological viewpoint we could dismiss any idea that God beckons us to tomorrow. We may believe that everything is predetermined by God and that we have no real choices about tomorrow, or we may admit that God does indeed invite us to a particular tomorrow and that we have a choice to say yes or no to that call.

Denying God's call to tomorrow is congruent with this postreligious age, in which what matters is what can be seen, heard, tasted, touched, or smelled. As this book is being written, much of the northern and western world is enjoying a long period of economic growth and stability. In such a time it is easy to forget faith and to depend on the dollar. Some speak of a spiritual revival, but for every active worshiper or stadium-prayer-rally attender there are hundreds who stay away because of other priorities. God calling us to tomorrow? The mind of today thinks, "What's in it for me?"

One approach says we have no choice but to accept the predetermined life that God has put into motion. Some biblical witnesses support this view. Jeremiah, for example, spoke of how God knew him and called him before his birth, meaning that Jeremiah had no choice but that which God had chosen for him (Jer. 1:4-5). St. Augustine of Hippo, great spiritual guide of the church, spoke of the "city of God" and the "city of man," and declared that those who aimed for one or the other had no choice about it. The great reformer John Calvin said that God predestines our lives and, indeed, the whole created order. Double predestination became a dominating theology of part of the reforming church, with its assertion that some were predestined to eternal punishment and others to eternal life, and though we would not be certain which path was ours until after death, we could not change it.

Most people of faith today do not hold to a theology of denial or of predeterminism. But vestiges of both creep into the faith community. In truth, neither offers direction for people of faith. Faced with the reality of change, we must grapple with the exciting truth that life for the church is also changing—and in rich, wonderful ways. In Hans Kung's words, "Today we do not want merely to go round in circles. It is absolutely necessary to free ourselves, to break out of the *one-dimensionality* [Kung's emphasis] of our modern existence, to 'transcend' it."[5]

How do we transcend our existence? There is no single, simple answer. Indeed, many postliberal religious thinkers are moving away from positing confidence in rational approaches to faith and placing their trust more in the mystery of God's presence and self-disclosure. To ask and open ourselves seriously to the question, "What is God calling us to do and be?" is not merely to ask, "What's around the next bend?" It is to risk a whole new life, to be willing to deny ourselves and the way we have seen the future in order to be drawn into a whole new way. Is this not what Jesus meant when he said, "If any want to become my followers, let them deny themselves . . . and follow me" (Mark 8:34)?

From an organizational point of view, asking about God's call leads to this third, anticipatory, way of moving into the future, this one called "proleptic." From the Greek word "prolepsis," which means, roughly, "anticipation," this way of viewing tomorrow celebrates the reality that God is out there as well as here, that we are called to move in God's direction. Yet God is ever patient and gracious and waits for us to move. God doesn't wait with divine arms crossed, tapping a foot and grunting in irritation at our slowness. "The word of God is living and active, sharper than any two-edged sword" (Heb. 4:12a), finding old and fresh ways to call and recall us to the future that is best and most fruitful for us. This way of positioning our lives for faithful movement in God's direction does not call for great spiritual virtuosity, but rather for openness and a willingness to hear and accept God's voice as it leads.

We can affirm from our faith certain beliefs and values rooted in biblical and traditional sources. These include being a church that tries to embody God's grace by embracing all sorts of people, of both genders and all ages, cultures, and ethnic histories; people who aren't compelled to be alike, who celebrate differences and honor individuals' particular gifts. Such a value says that we are, "red and yellow, black and white," that all are equally precious in God's sight. While not every congregation will be this inclusive in its composition, it is as though every congregation would be willing to include everyone in the world if challenged to do so.

In sum, we are not just sitting here on this massive ball in space waiting for the future to happen to us. To whatever extent possible, we are called to say yes to God's call to listen and act faithfully to join in making this Earth a place as alive in spirit as it is in physical reality.

God does have a future for us. If we agree with this statement, then what does this assent ask of clergy? As the church changes, pastors cannot react passively to all that is happening.

A 12-year informal assessment I conducted of just under 100 congregations shows them falling into three quite distinct groups: vital and changing, resistant to change and new programming, and passive and unresponsive in either direction.

The most important learning from this assessment was that the pastor's role, whether perceived as influential or powerless, was nonetheless one of the pivotal factors in every congregation. Where the pastor was energized, willing to lead and enable the congregation to plan and celebrate change, then the congregation became a place of hope. Where the pastor was either controlling or yielded control to a few laypersons who then treated the pastor as a hireling, change was resisted and nothing new happened. Where the pastor served primarily as a chaplain with no role at all in the corporate life of the congregation save to preach theologically unthreatening sermons, then the congregation was passive about the future. Certainly some of these congregations placed their ministers in whichever of these styles prevailed. But whether through the minister's initiative or that of the congregation, the minister's affect, or impact, was one of the critical factors in the congregations' vitality.

Certainly the pastors of creative churches will acknowledge their need for new skills, for redefinition of their roles as the church enters a time of unprecedented change. All three categories of congregations mentioned above must come to understand their changing roles, or the church will die beneath them.

CHAPTER 3

The Burdens We Carry

Go on your way. See, I am sending you out like lambs into the midst of wolves. Carry no purse, no bag, no sandals.

(Jesus' words in Luke 10:3-4a)

This idea of traveling light, of going into mission without even sandals on our feet, much less a bag filled with essentials, may be a grand one, but it's one that seems impossible on the face of it. As the child of overseas missionaries, I can tell you that it was an exciting time when my family packed for a term of service in Africa. Even more exhilarating was the arrival of a semi-annual order of groceries or clothing and household goods. Living in a remote outpost, we found moments like these, when baggage was our focus, to be among the great times of our lives. Even my parents, who took seriously their call to self-denying service, would get excited when the goods came. "Carry no purse, no bag, no sandals." What would Jesus think of our exhilaration at packing for life in the Congo? Is this what his admonition was about? Or was he speaking metaphorically, urging followers to live uncluttered with other interests, free to attend only to what allowed one to be a faithful servant?

Like everyone else, clergy carry burdens with them. These may be like bags, stuffed with skills, convictions, hopes, and dreams. They may be lined with fears and doubts about one's capacity to fulfill one's calling. They might be gorged with satisfied self-absorption and an inability to listen actively to feedback, evaluation, and critique. And those bags may contain the results of years of wear and tear and woundedness, as well as loads of unrealistic expectations and demands of parishioners, denominational systems, and communities whose wants we could never fully meet.

I am interested here in exploring particular stuff we may be carrying that results from the intensity of our times. We need to know what fills or frazzles us, because we can't expect to eject this baggage automatically as we fly across the frontier to a new ministry or millennium.

Before looking at the particular burdens of clergy, it may be useful to examine the place of religion and the church in the 20th-to-21st century culture.

A Culture of Disregard

It is widely understood that the past century of religion in American life has not been one of prosperity and growth, as many would like to believe. Indeed, most mainline denominations—those churches that have been part of the landscape for most of this nation's life—experienced their greatest growth in the last two decades of the 1800s and the first decade of the 20th century. In my denomination, the Christian Church (Disciples of Christ), the majority of congregations in existence today were formed during that 30-year span.

We have fooled ourselves into thinking that most of the 20th century was a time of growth and cultural expansion. In reality, many congregations were experiencing stable and productive lives, but burgeoning growth was no longer taking place. During a brief interlude in the 1950s, say Wade Clark Roof and William McKinney, "the established institutions . . . enjoyed an almost artificial prosperity."[1] The very churches that grew in numbers and popularity also became "something of a culture-religion," captive to middle-class values and lacking "in their ability to sustain a strong transcendent vision."[2] Liberal and mainline churches became so bonded to the culture that their ways of thinking and acting became indistinguishable from it.

But this identity changed as battles for civil rights, peace, sexual equality, and the rights of homosexuals and bisexuals erupted. Churches that had reflected the supposed majority culture diminished in influence. And some of yesterday's culture-bound churches found God calling them to courageous acts that looked the culture in the face and said, "No!"

In retrospect, the growth and prosperity of the 1950s were a post-war "blip." Indeed, organized (especially mainline) churches and religion in general had been steadily diminishing in numbers and influence through the first half of the 20th century.

As we enter a new century and millennium, we are faced with a culture of disregard—by which I mean one that neither supports nor opposes the church. If this were not so, persecution of people for their faith would be of greater concern. It is happening in many parts of the world, often at the hands of opponents who claim faith as their justification. Certainly this is not the first era when such evil has been committed by forces ostensibly motivated by religious belief. What frightens us is that such evil deeds draw little attention.

Ours is a culture in which religion is essentially disregarded. Paradoxically, in some ways it would be preferable to see religion scorned. Religion's status as an acceptable part of the woodwork is more difficult to cope with than its being demeaned and belittled.

This is the cultural context in which many pastors must serve. It has been years since religion had such an impact that landmark legislation like the Civil Rights Act of 1964 could be passed largely because, as Senator Richard Russell, leader of the opposition, said, the galleries were loaded with clergy. In many communities clergy aren't even invited to give invocations at civic functions anymore. (For some pastors this may be a blessing.) And while para-church movements such as the Promise Keepers have given some new visibility to religion, established institutions of religion continue to become less important to society in general.

Most mainline denominations have been losing members steadily for more than three decades. Some put the best face on statistics by reporting that losses have diminished for several years in succession. Parishes are aging, both in the age of individual parishioners and in years of parish existence. The changes brought by aging were summed up well for me ten years ago when a stalwart middle-aged member of a large congregation in a southern city said that none of his and his contemporaries' children still participated in the life of that parish, though many lived in the area. A handful were involved in other congregations, with a few in new, conservative mega-churches. But most had left any form of organized religion. If they left in rebellion, they stayed away because their loyalty was claimed by jobs, family, hobbies, and other consuming pursuits. In a typical week an average of 50 to 60 U.S. Protestant parishes disappear. They may close by their own decision, merge, or find themselves closed by their denomination.[3]

The loss of public confidence in the church and clergy can be seen in data from the Gallup organization. Until the late 1980s, "organized religion" enjoyed the most confidence of any institution in the public's view. At that time about two in three Americans said that the church was an institution in which they placed utmost trust. By 1995 the military and the police had moved ahead of the church and organized religion in confidence levels. Until 1975, as much as 68 percent of the public placed organized religion at the top of the list. By 1995 that figure had fallen to 57 percent. During the ten years from 1985 to 1995 the percentage of people who "would rate the honesty and ethical standards of clergy as very high (first)" dropped from 66 percent to 56 percent. Druggists moved ahead of clergy in the confidence rating.[4]

It could be argued that the change was fueled largely by the televangelism scandals. But to leave it at that is to oversimply. Much of the change reflects ways in which religious institutions and clergy have presented themselves to the public. When asked what kind of job religious leaders have been doing in raising the nation's moral and ethical standards, 36 percent of respondents said good, 50 percent said fair, and 12 percent said poor. But when asked how much influence they think religious leaders *could* have in raising the nation's moral and ethical standards, 68 percent said "a great deal," 27 percent said "some," and only 4 percent said "not much."[5] Clearly an expectation is not being met, and hope persists that more could be done.

Shall we flail ourselves for these statistics? By no means. The polls mirror perceptions, and in a society more complex than the apparently simple one in which the pastor was the "main man in town" (few pastors were female), it is too easy to say that the clergy aren't exerting the influence they did.

Yet pastors are often the first to feel the impact of this disregard, which can leave them feeling powerless. From the Sunday morning soccer leagues of suburbia to competing causes that lead people to make the church just one more option, the culture of disregard leaves pastors with little influence. Some are prominent in their communities by dint of hard work, which may be a positive development. Rather than having influence handed to them, it may be that pastors *should* labor to earn it.

Among older church members who regret the decline of religious influence, nostalgia takes over. I tire of hearing the words: "Things began to go bad when they took God out of the schools." I want to reply that in those days schools and public facilities were rigidly segregated, women had few opportunities, town populations were defined by who lived on which side of the tracks, and across the southern half of the world massive numbers were suffering under European colonialism. It wasn't such a great time after all, was it?

In fact, some religious groups were strong separatists. As a matter of principle, they didn't teach or practice religion in their schools. The daughter of a Lutheran pastor told me how Missouri Synod and Wisconsin Synod Lutherans operated their schools this way. All signs indicate that their communities and schools were no worse off than those where public religion was imposed.

But it does no good to rail against nostalgia and thus plant the seeds of even more defensiveness about the past. Rather, what is called for is a fresh understanding of the call and role of the ministry. We look now at some of those burdens today's clergy carry into the new century.

Conflicting Expectations and Demands

Once when several colleagues and I in judicatory ministries of oversight took a public stand in opposition to capital punishment, the resulting mail I received, while certainly not fan mail, was nonetheless instructive. By far the majority came from people who supported the death penalty and, in various ways, took us to task:

"It's the only way to get justice."
"They deserve to die."
"It serves the victims' families."
"You religious people are meddling in matters that you have no business in!"

No amount of argument would stem the tide of letters or the flood of convictions. But one response, from the pastor of a large and quite conservative congregation of my own tradition, gave me pause. He said, "I thank you for doing that. You can say things that I cannot say. I am not sure I agree with everything you and your friends said, but we need you to do this because you can and I can't."

It was a poignant statement about the expectations—indeed, the demands—under which this faithful parish pastor served. On one hand, his congregation wanted him to teach morality to members and their children. On the other hand, many of his parishioners would be quick to call him to account for utterances on moral issues that brought their own convictions into question. Other parishioners no doubt had different and conflicting expectations. Meeting the expectations of some would necessarily mean failing to meet others'!

Pastors may or may not be aware of others' expectations. But most situations are not as loaded with the potential for conflicting judgments as this one. Church members have expectations about how the pastor spends her time, whether he visits enough, if she is going to too many meetings, or if he is trying to manage matters best left to the laity.

Mundane issues? Surely. Yet we dare not diminish their importance. A pile of little stinky pieces can fill a whole bucket with garbage that, left unattended, will reek. The consequences of ignoring such issues can be messy and unpleasant. Though one should recognize the emergence of a major matter, many crises erupt from an accumulation of smaller issues.

Pastor Paul had been at Our Saviour Church for just under two years. He had succeeded the founding pastor of this exciting young congregation, now just ten years old. What church leaders hadn't told him before he arrived was the effect on Our Saviour of the region's economic slowdown. A number of major leaders had been forced to leave the area just five years into the congregation's life. Add to that the reality of the denominational and cultural expectations that the new church should buy property and erect a building as soon as possible. Isn't "If you build it, they will come" a driving maxim for starting new congregations? (Admittedly, this catchphrase gained currency from the film *Field of Dreams* later than the construction of most of those churches.) The congregation did get its bricks and mortar, but at the cost of time and talent that might have been spent building spiritual depth, community strength, biblical intelligence, and the organizational skill to cope with tough and tender occasions. In one sense, though, members did their work well, for they met expectations.

Ten years later, crisis hit—after the organizing pastor had resigned in despair, still pained by the departure of supportive pioneers; after new people had come in from a different tradition without grasping the implications of serving in a new church (after all, by then Our Saviour had land, a lovely building, and a full-time pastor), and after the new pastor came. Pastor Paul was a blunt man. He preferred to "call it like it is."

Sometimes he cursed. A good preacher, he was not as thorough an ad-
ministrator as some expected their pastor to be. He didn't spend a lot of
time doing what he called "dinky pastoral stuff."

And then an antagonist came into the congregation.[6] She saw all
these separate signs of disarray waiting for someone to collect them.
She did just that for a year or so, and then, gathering the friends she had
made, just about demolished Pastor Paul.

The expectations that come a pastor's way can concern beliefs, behaviors, idiosyncrasies, anything that looks or feels wrong to a parishio-
ner, or any demand made on the pastor's or congregation's life.

What makes these expectations particularly burdensome for pastors
at the end of the 20th century is an "in-your-face" culture, where in-
sistence on getting one's way becomes a driving force for action. Early
in the 1980s Robert Bellah and colleagues conducted a landmark study
of what motivates people to caring acts. *Habits of the Heart*,[7] named for
a phrase from Alexis de Tocqueville's study of American life in the early
19th century, entailed intensive research with several dozen Americans.
The findings were unsettling. The best of deeds were often found to be
done because they made the doer feel good. In this secular society, if
even good is done to benefit the doer, it is hard to refute the conclusion
that pretty much everything else is done in self-interest as well. Though
"getting one's way" sounds self-centered, and "feeling good" seems
harmless, they are two poles on the continuum of self-interest. Even
good deeds can serve as a means of getting one's way.

This phenomenon has meaning for pastors, particularly as they enable people to receive the benefits of faithful service. Do we encourage
people to serve because it will make them feel good? And what of the
pastor's own service? Where is his or her reward? This is becoming a
larger issue as Baby-Boomers become the leaders in congregations.

Added to the conflicting, sometimes unrealistic expectations of
others are the pastor's self-expectations. These may conflict with the
expectations of others. As a pastor to pastors, one of the more painful
processes I have witnessed occurs when a pastor, fresh out of seminary,
goes to a first parish, or when a more experienced pastor begins a new
ministry. Both are normally times of renewal and rekindling of vocational devotion. Armed with strong self-expectations, wanting to serve
with competence and dedication, this new servant begins to experience
a world in which his or her gifts, graces, and skills are not necessarily
those others want.

While self/other differences can cause stress, the greater stress often comes from within, as the pastor finds those high self-expectations diminished and enters a time when what he or she wants to do is erased in the face of the members' expectations. For example, the pastor, skilled in pastoral counseling, may find that the congregation wants only routine visiting of people who do not or cannot come to worship. Another pastor, who wants to engage in a teaching ministry, may find that despite every effort otherwise, most members want Sunday school only for the children. By the grace of God this mismatch of gifts and expectations doesn't happen in every situation. But where it does, the pastor's internal expectations can be deflated and defeated. The outcome is poor performance, depression, bitterness, and despair over both the congregation's life and the pastor's vocation.

In addition, members' lives have become far more complex in recent decades. For example, economic demands often require two parents to work. Demands on pastors have grown accordingly. Volunteers have less time than in earlier years. Families' needs are more acute. Decisions, such as about church finances or who to help with the church's benevolence resources, must now be shared or even sometimes made by clergy alone, simply because many laypersons are not as available to make these decisions. This has been happening while changing social justice laws are placing more demands on the church to receive, feed, house, clothe, and counsel the poor. It is no wonder that demands on and expectations of the pastor have grown. And when expectations are in conflict, how should the pastor respond?

Increased expectations can lead to pain. The best response is not to attempt meeting all expectations and demands, to make everyone happy. To do so would be like living at the entrance of a black hole in space where everything gets sucked in and lost. The appropriate response is to live by a disciplined and focused style of ministry that will enable people to see beyond their demands to a greater purpose and hope.

The Pain Pastors Feel

Many of those who genuinely sense God's call to a vocation of service have always felt some degree of pain. Some feel others' pain, and they feel pain for that which they themselves have given up. The prophet

Jeremiah sat down by the side of the road one day and said, "Cursed be the day on which I was born! The day when my mother bore me, let it not be blessed!" (Jer. 20:14). Having had a snoot full of the deference and defiance of both kings and commoners in Israel, the prophet believed for a few minutes that he was in the wrong place. At that moment his pain was more than he could bear. That this point did not mark the end of Jeremiah's ministry is understandable. Many people called by God have been healed and helped back to vital witness after time spent in despair. The task of this book is not to eradicate the forces that can cause despair, but to promote understanding.

Many years ago, during times of radical racial upheavals, at a ministers' retreat for our judicatory, I was paired with two colleagues for an information-sharing exercise that asked us to speak frankly about our ministries. I reeled out all the wonderful things happening where I served as pastor. Finally my colleagues had heard enough. With what seemed one voice, they said, "Can't you be honest with us? Why do you act as though nothing mean and bad ever happens there?" Called so bluntly to honesty, I began remembering: There was the time I'd heard that 94 people were prepared to leave because of my preaching about civil rights, or the rumors spread when I was seen in a public demonstration advising an integrated youth group, or the objections many had to a space-leasing arrangement we were considering with Operation Headstart. I had allowed myself to become numb to real pain.

People called to pastoral ministry are often likely to overlook their pain. Somewhere in the pathway of preparation we learn a subtle lesson about stoicism, about bearing up with equilibrium and poise no matter what may invade us. My experience was, I suspect, more typical than uncommon.

The troubling results: first, we ignore pains that will hurt, defeat, and even kill us if they are allowed to fester and grow. Second, our vocation is cheated if we don't learn and grow from all experience, including pain. Few pastors have only negative experiences. Just as rare are those whose entire careers are positive.

Not all clergy will feel the depths of pain described here, but for each pastor there may be some word or thought here that fits the pattern of a personal experience.

Emotional pain is caused by a variety of circumstances, but in my experience, the deepest pain comes when certain processes are set in motion: when the pastor's competence is questioned, when his or her integrity is attacked, or when support systems are undeveloped or undermined.

Questioning Competence

The extent of preparation required for the practice of pastoral ministry makes competence important. In times past the clergy may have been the best educated and most highly regarded authorities in the community. In my denomination's earlier rural history the "county seat church" was an important institution. Until the mid-20th century, a large, visible, influential church quite often stood on the town square. Sometimes space was made for several mainline congregations to occupy similar places of importance in the county seat town. Generally a midwestern and southern phenomenon, the power accorded these institutions and their pastors often was sufficient to allow limitations in the clergy's training and skill to be overlooked. Pastors were simply assumed to be competent.

Although pastors' inadequacies were perhaps more easily ignored 50 years ago, clergy today are not necessarily better and more capable, though they are generally at least as well-trained and competent. Further, the pastor is no longer one of the best-educated people in town, or even in the congregation. The culture has long been moving from a stance that allowed the church to be the community's anchor. In today's vast cultural sprawl, the superhighway, the shopping mall, and the computer terminal are the anchor places of life. Here the pastor does not function with that same built-in guarantee of respect.

Moreover, people in church are pulled in many more ways. As a result, the pastor's ability to carry out her calling is subject to far more scrutiny than in earlier times. Such sources of competition as media religion, professional counseling centers, and varieties of organized activities for children and youth abound. Multiple methods for avoiding boredom are available. Some, like the video game room at the mall, make the church's capacity to attract people more critical than ever. "Average" stimulation just won't attract people anymore.

While it is not fair, it is a fact that if the church appears to be losing this battle, the pastor's competence may be called into question. "If the pastor could only preach better" or "didn't pray so long, the church might attract more worshipers."

It is still true that most congregations are small, with one pastor. While there is a movement to begin using the gifts of the laity in more creative ways, massive demands are still placed on pastors to do everything well. Because many smaller congregations face threats to their survival, the pastor's performance is spotlighted even more sharply.

Under such pressure it is not rare for the pastor's competence to be questioned by others and even by the pastor herself. When time comes to fix blame for seemingly uncontrollable events, the most visible person is the easiest target. No small number of pastors have lost their positions because of this visibility. Some congregations habitually resort to an overused solution: when things go wrong, get rid of the pastor and maybe that will fix it all. One church repeated this ritual every 3 years for more than 20 years. Only when one pastor refused to allow them to violate her so blatantly, having found the God-given courage to confront these forces, did the congregation undergo a systemic change that rid them of this terrible habit and brought about spiritual renewal.

As with this remarkable example, it is possible for pastors to respond to the questioning of their competence with faith and self-confidence, thus bringing to the congregation a living gift of word and service. This kind of leadership can lift people from pettiness to purposeful community in God's name.

Attacks on Integrity

Attacks on integrity can be far more devastating and painful than challenges to competence. Clergy still live in glass houses, though the pastoral residence may no longer stand at the center of town. That people still watch and evaluate pastors and their families, even in a culture of disregard, puzzles some. Yet it is understandable because of the fragile character of congregations. Though not the center of community adulation as before, the pastor is still a model for the behavior of others. Indeed, example is still the most lasting way of teaching.

A good leader will not ask of others anything he or she is not willing to do. No strong leader leads from the sidelines. This doesn't mean that every leader must march out in front and get muddier and bloodier than anyone else. But the real leader communicates a willingness to do so if necessary. We will return to a discussion of leadership later in this book, but suffice it for now to say that pastors are expected to be examples, for thus we teach. It is a realistic expectation.

Integrity has a number of meanings, one of which is the consistency between what we say and what we do. Following through on promises made, saying the same thing to different people about an incident, and generating excitement by setting an example, are all ways of showing this consistency. This virtue is at the heart of the pastor's role as leader. If questions are raised about this consistency, integrity is clouded. If the questioners are believed, the leader's role can be called into question.

The ways to attack the pastor's integrity range from sending anonymous mail to giving him the silent treatment. Several times, when I have intervened to seek conflict resolution in a congregation, I have declared that the telephone changed the face of congregational conflict. This is particularly true when a conflict about the pastor's integrity is fueled by gossip and innuendo. In pre-telephone days conflicts didn't light up the ecclesiastical switchboard as they do now. The more accessible our means of communicating, the easier it is to miscommunicate, to share inaccurate, unfair information, as well as the straight stuff.

Pastors are so vulnerable to this kind of abuse that when a pastor does make a mistake, it amounts to an invitation to a bashing. Fortunately many congregations and their lay leaders try to deal with a pastor's mistakes with fairness. But some don't, and pastors and congregations are hurt.

The diminished trust that comes from questioning the pastor's integrity is the source of some of the greatest pain experienced by pastors:

"They act like they don't believe anything I say anymore."
"They won't bring their kids here."
"They say I lie, and I can't stand it. It is so wrong."
"They are talking all around town, and it's all untrue."

Such are the wrenching words I have heard from pastors whose trust was wrongly questioned.

Healing broken souls is work that only God can do, though God is helped by supportive and caring colleagues and friends, and we who serve in "oversight" ministries can do much more. Calling the congregation, and in particular the persons responsible, to account is work that the church must be willing to do. There are times when the pastor's integrity is and should be under fire because of his or her words and deeds. More often than not, however, the attack is launched because someone didn't like the pastor's actions and chose to fight dirty. The pain is too searing, the consequences too damaging for the church to ignore such occasions.

Here is a place where the role of ministries of oversight is crucial. These ministers can work in three ways: (1) as pastors to pastors, (2) as pastors to pastor-congregation relationships, or (3) as both. (Of course, some judicatory executives choose to function as bureaucrats, rather than be "hobbled" by pastoral duties.) Judicatory pastors need to be intentional about performing both pastoral functions if the pain of pastors is to be heard and helped.

Inadequate Support Systems

Support systems are essential for a pastor's continuing health. Many pastors are, for various reasons, loners. It's easy to fall into going it alone because there aren't many pastors around. It's out of the ordinary to be a pastor in this culture. There is good reason for clergy to wonder: Who but another ordained minister really *does* understand us? There are other reasons why some choose not to relate to others. Among these might be fear that others will think me inadequate, or that someone else will be "better" and I will be unmasked. Some pastors believe they are less than competent in some areas of their work, and they would rather not be "discovered." Sometimes they are right. Some believe that other people don't care about them or what they do. For many pastors there is just enough truth in these beliefs for life to be scary. Sometimes it *does* seem that pastors are the favored targets of people determined to get their way. Some pastors choose to isolate themselves and carry their self-doubts privately. Often, however, the pastor really *is* alone, but not by choice.

Not too many people outside the ranks of professional church work understand the particular dynamics of ministry. Even the most alert and sensitive laity seldom comprehend the demands on, and hopes of, their pastor. Because the agreement between pastor and parishioners requires the pastor to seek to know and care for them, but does not require them to know or even care about the pastor, clergy live on a one-way street so far as emotional support is concerned.

That said, it is fortunately true that many laypeople do care genuinely for their pastors. Heroic laypeople will support the clergy under almost any circumstances, out of deep regard for the office, or because they make it a point to know and love their pastor and family.

But too often these people are a minority. Others revert to that pastor-parish agreement when personal or congregational stress builds to the point of distress, or when the normal working balance is pushed to the point where "adaptability is impaired."[8] A willingness to trust may give way to a cold expectation that the pastor must do what he or she was hired to do. Contracts become more important than relationships.

Too often laypeople consider the pastor no more than a hireling. Though such members may be small in number, they can also be so small in spirit that they carry great potential for destruction. In the end, most pastors find little lasting support among laypeople.

Nor is it always easy for pastors to seek support from colleagues, particularly if the colleagues represent potential competition. Because it is difficult for many clergy to acknowledge their own vulnerability and pain, collegial ties may be one of the most threatening linkages to cultivate.

The most obvious support system for the pastor, the family—a household family, intimate friends, or the family at the other end of the phone—is not always an easy place to ask for support. When a pastor works long hours, remains on call day and night, and must be away from home at times when other families are together, it is not easy to ask the family to be a source of comfort. For some, the instinct may be to keep on giving at home just as on the job. But far too many have given everything to their work, leaving nothing for the family. So assurance of family support is not as obvious as it might appear.

Because the pastor is called to be a caregiver, it may not be easy to be cared for. In research conducted more than 15 years ago to gain information about long pastorates, an Alban Institute team discovered that nearly all pastors who served longer than eight years in the same parish were "intuitive-feeling" in temperament. This term, from the Myers-Briggs Type Indicator,[9] describes persons who gather data and then assess information by their own best sense of things, and who then make decisions based on their values and what they think people will want and need, rather than by logic. Analytical judgments are not likely to be made by people of this temperament. Such people are not apt to spend much time receiving help. Giving comes more naturally. Thus when under stress, when needy and seeking, it may well be difficult for the "intuitive-feeling" pastor to ask for help. Ideally each pastor will have four sources of continuing personal and professional support:

- Family: With strong mutual relationships, the pastor supports and is supported.

- Colleagues: In one or more active and regular configurations, one's problems and hopes, dilemmas and possibilities can be shared and compared, and solutions sought.

- Parishioners, particularly those on such committees as pastoral relations and personnel: In committees, at least in theory, the means of support are institutionalized and well managed. All support from parishioners depends on a climate of clear trust and feedback so the people and pastor can exchange affection, fun, critique, and help when it is needed.

- Spiritual sources: Without spiritual undergirding there will be no life and hope in this ministry, even if all the other sources of support appear to be in place. We will return to this topic later.

Support systems may be lacking either because the available ones aren't tended, or because they were never developed to begin with.

When a pastor is under severe stress, support systems can be among the most reliable sources of help or the first casualties of the crisis. Ironically many pastors under heavy pressure withdraw from support systems, not wanting those to whom they normally turn knowing they have weaknesses that this distress can reveal. Some laity tend to view the Pastor/Parish Relations Committee as existing *only* for times of trouble. Some clergy avoid dealing with crises, while some laity treat every little conflict as a crisis. But the truth is, if formal church support systems are used only during difficult times, the systems will always fail. They must be nurtured in the good times if they are to be accessible and of any value during difficulties.

The importance of support cannot be overemphasized. But support for the pastor has to include some components that are deliberately nurtured. Some can be colleague support groups, spiritual guidance, and regularly scheduled education opportunities. Relationships in which difficulties can be admitted, where counsel can be sought, where simple acceptance (grace) is present, where one can be pressed to learn and grow—all are essential to a pastor's health. The extent to which we avoid such relationships can be seen as a measure of our own sense of insecurity in this demanding vocation to which God has called us.

When Spiritual Life Is Fragile

To meet new role expectations, pastors must be rooted in rich and strong spirituality. Too often, though, pastors feel powerless, without authority, and unable to fulfill expected roles. Often enough, there is a companion sense of spiritual emptiness. We believe ourselves truly called by God, we get prepared, and then we feel ourselves without strength to do the work. Why?

Sometimes these feelings arise because clergy are in a very visible vocation. While her world doesn't always listen, it surely looks. Little may be made of venture capitalists who commit billions of dollars in crimes against other stockholders. But a church worker, particularly an ordained one, is big news if a discrepancy of a few thousand dollars is discovered, and certainly if there are other hints of moral lapses. Religious people, beginning with the clergy, are increasingly the targets of large lawsuits for many reasons. Many suits prove to be frivolous, but they can, nonetheless, lead clergy to such feelings of discouragement that spiritual life becomes empty. While spiritual emptiness should never be construed as an excuse, such sinful and abusive behaviors as sexual misconduct often happen because of a lack of significant spiritual discipline—a chronic reality among too many clergy in our times.

Lack of spiritual discipline, and a resulting emptiness, can have other causes as well:

Pastoral ministry is a busy vocation. The demands that raise our levels of stress make time such a precious commodity that little is reserved for prayer and other spiritual practices. Lack of knowledge of spiritual practices may keep us from growing in a way that will equip us for increasing role demands. An inclination to say yes to all requests results in a failure to set priorities and pay attention to our own needs.

What will help us? Barney McLaughlin, an experienced spiritual teacher and guide, offers an understanding of spirituality that has meaning. Spirituality is the place "where God's voice and our actions intersect." There are countless ways in which God speaks to us.[10] Prayer, worship, the Bible, other readings, music and other arts, the faith community, dialogue, historical events that are shaped by ethical concerns, creation as seen most clearly in the uncluttered-by-humans world of nature, the simplicity of little children, healing—these are but some of the ways in which we "hear" a word from God that is from outside our routine thoughts and experiences. We need to ask what difference will this make in the ways we do things? Will it change our behavior? Will it make a difference in our lives?

Spirituality, understood this way, is not an abstraction that may or may not be relevant but the actual experience of God's word meeting our actions and affecting our reactions to life. Spiritual experience is part of the life of the faithful, applicable to experience, not a special realm occupied by some who are blessed in unusual ways. Dutch-born author-priest Henri Nouwen, best known for his writings on spirituality, said:

> For the mystic as well as revolutionary, life means breaking through the veil covering our human existence and following the vision that has become manifest to us. Whatever we call this vision. . .we still believe that conversion and revolution alike derive their power from a source beyond the limitations of our own createdness.[11]

That "vision" makes a difference in how we live and work, play and relate to others. To experience this interaction with God in our lives, we need to be ready, open, waiting. Spiritual disciplines can support this stance of readiness, or what the American monk and writer Thomas Merton called:

> the darkness . . . [the] nothingness [in which] he sees all his works come to nothing, for he is overwhelmed by the activity of God's immense love, and by the fruitive inclination of his Spirit he . . . becomes one spirit with God.[12]

Under great pressure, when, as Canadian physician and research scientist Hans Selye puts it, "stress becomes distress,"[13] we clergy may tend to pay less attention to spiritual resources and place more reliance on our own reserves.

Describing a time of conflict and crisis, Beecher Hicks, in his book *Preaching Through the Storm*, tells about the place of preaching in difficult times: "The storm provides an unnatural, alien, even hostile environment in which preaching with power can become nearly impossible." [14] To his statement, it might be added that praying, studying, counseling, administering, and almost any other functions of the pastor's ministry "with power" become nearly impossible. For Hicks, for more than 20 years pastor of Metropolitan Baptist Church, Washington, D.C., one of the largest and most influential African-American Baptist churches in America, the conflict emerged during a building program whose aim was to be faithful in seeking to do God's will. Unanticipated opposition created unprecedented crisis and stress. Hicks' capacity to do what he did so well was challenged. That such a God-gifted servant would be thus spiritually confronted suggests that few of us will not also feel daunted when faced with "the storm."

One of history's lessons is that people turn to those with an authoritative word in difficult times. Yet when matters are most difficult, people most often ignore clergy in contemporary religious institutions. Even some of the very people who call us to be spiritually grounded, the members of our congregations, may look to other sources for strength when strength seems most needed, choosing coping methods that appear to offer immediate satisfaction while demanding less than would be the case with deep spirituality. A quick fix is often more alluring than a spiritual growth process that will call for change.

One possible reason for this tendency: If the church is caught up in crisis, the clergy will probably be put in the middle of it. Whether the crisis is of their doing, clergy will be blamed, commended, attacked, or lauded. Such characterizations can make it difficult for pastors to be spiritual resources and leaders to an institution in trauma.

A result can be the diminishing of the pastor's own spiritual strength. If the pastor is not engaged in regular disciplines of spiritual life, a period of distress can be truly unsettling. Because stress exhausts us, the time, energy, creativity, and curiosity needed to seek and pursue fresh forms of spiritual nurture are not present. The struggle for survival saps our energy.

This is not the place for an exhaustive listing and description of spiritual development resources. Suffice it to say that the pastor who does not pray, meditate, reflect, write, study, listen, run, sing, or make use of any other spiritual exercises will be ill-fitted for a storm.

There is a point beyond which high stress can make whatever spiritual disciplines we practice seem irrelevant. For now we must say that many pastors find their spirituality the first casualty of a time of great distress in congregational life, whether caused by conflicting demands, pain, attacks on integrity, or the loss of support systems.

Consequences of the Burdens We Bring

Before we move into a prescriptive examination of the future, we need to consider the consequences and casualties of the climate that exists in much of today's religious world. We have discussed the culture's general shrug at organized religion, conflicting expectations, the pain pastors experience, and spiritual distress. Where do these negative elements leave pastors?

Probably the greatest single area of crisis is in the number of clergy who are fired. *Leadership* magazine, in 1996, published results of a national survey of Protestant clergy in which 23 percent indicated they had been fired at least once, and 43 percent of these said a small faction or power group forced them out. The survey also showed that 41 percent of congregations who fired the pastor had earlier fired at least two others. Pastors most often cited personality conflicts as the reason for the firing (43 percent). Other reasons included conflicting visions (17 percent), congregational finances (7 percent), moral malfeasance (5 percent), and unrealistic expectations (4 percent).[15] (One wonders what reasons lay leaders might have given for these same firings.)

While these numbers may seem high, clergy who have been fired may be more likely to answer such a survey than those who have not. Still, the statistics are alarming. Particularly distressing are the numbers of congregations that have fired more than one or two pastors. My observation as a middle judicatory pastor-with-oversight is that certain congregations cannot get away from their overused solutions to problems, and the more the same solutions are used, the less likely they are to solve anything. In many situations where pastors have been fired, the problems did not go away with the pastor.

Other troubling results exist as well. G. Lloyd Rediger, in *Clergy Killers*,[16] shares data from his own counseling. "(In) my counseling with pastors since 1970 the numbers in each category have grown from near zero to the figures listed."

Burnout (exhaustion to the point of malfunction)
  • clergy: 15%
  • general population: 8-12%

Divorce (once or more)
  • clergy: 15% (much higher in some denominations)
  • general population: 30-40%

Chemically dependent (professional impairment through use of alcohol, etc.)
  • clergy: 5%
  • general population: 10-12%

Mental disorder (inability to function normally)
  • clergy: 2%
  • general population: 8-10%

Moral malfeasance (immorality)
  • clergy: 10%
  • other helping professions: 12-15%

While these data come from one counselor, they likely, because of his length and depth of experience, come close to reflecting the population. One person seeking information about clergy sexual misconduct said it is probably too soon to know the extent of this crisis, for though denominations are rapidly, though belatedly, equipping themselves to deal appropriately with such misconduct, church officials often refuse to disclose numbers for fear of violating privacy laws.

The picture painted by this brief statistical summary is not pretty. It leaves us with concern about the health of many pastors. Add to these tangible problems such plagues as loneliness, pastors' families in pain, refusal to seek help, lack of self-care, financial shortages and lack of financial management skills, and we see a sad scene.

   Certainly not all pastors are trapped in such dilemmas. But even those not so caught find themselves on the receiving end of cultural pressures and conflicting expectations. They may not have acted out their stresses in ways that hurt themselves and others, but still they face what seems an uphill battle. We turn now to an exploration of a significant group of pastors who are finding ways to move ahead with hope, facing stresses and burdens faithfully, and coming out ahead.

CHAPTER 4

Exploring Prototypes

*Now faith is the assurance of things hoped for, the conviction of
things not seen.*
Indeed, by faith our ancestors received approval.

(Heb. 11:1-2)

Having examined conditions in the religious world of today, we now
ask, what about tomorrow? What will it be like?

A basic premise of this inquiry is that the future builds on the past,
though we don't always acknowledge it. Should we not, though, yearn
for a future that builds on the *best* of the past? How do we decide where
to go? Do we name our dreams and then go with the most enticing? Or
should we base our future on trends and methods that have proved most
successful in the past? If this is the way we go, how do we define success?

When we think about the future, our planning reflects the kind of
future we hope for. The process should be a prototype of the desired
outcome, the future we seek. A prototype is an exemplar, a model for
future development.

Fortunately, we can find such prototypes in pastors and congregations that are already stepping out in faith and taking new risks to do
God's work. These are the best exemplars or models for the future.

This is a time to break from the past, wait and listen for God, and
in this way seek guidance about moving into the future.

For my study I set out to find places in today's church where tomorrow is already being lived. I found two powerful realities: churches that
are growing (as we will see, growth is a multifaceted reality in vital
congregations) and congregations that are bold, courageous, and profoundly faithful in their way of seeing tomorrow. By the power of God's
Spirit, they are dreaming great dreams.

That faithfulness is expressed in a confessional theology that says to God: *Break me, melt me, mold me, fill me, use me.* Those first words, "break me," are not part of Daniel Iverson's well-known devotional song, "Spirit of the Living God." It isn't easy to own our need to be broken before we are re-formed. In many American churches we are still affected by a raw frontier confidence that says, "We can do it ourselves." In my research I heard pastors and churches going a step beyond—saying in effect, "What we have done has not been adequate. Break us, shatter our self-assurance, our belief that we have the best way, our mode of doing things the comfortable way we've always had. Bring us to the cross, where we, seeing our Lord dying there for us, will know that to live we must first die."

Before I began my research, I thought I would find clever programs, exciting strategies, motivational methods, and hot theologies designed to reach the unreached. Instead I found men and women who believe God wants them in ministry and who spare no effort in sharing that call with their parishes and the world beyond.

Let us turn now to the congregational life cycle and growth models and consider how the prototype congregations see themselves. We will then examine the critical elements of a vital congregation.

The Congregational Life Cycle

Congregations do not just spring up and live out their lives aimlessly, randomly. A wondrous movement takes place in the life of God's gathered people. From the earliest days of covenantal gatherings related in the Old Testament, this movement has been a reality. While no two communities of faith are identical, the broad stokes of the changing stages of congregational life are alike. Moving through this congregational life cycle does not imply getting better. It simply describes a sequence of changes.

Each of the 32 prototype congregations stands at some point in this life cycle. These 32 are not "Super Congregations" that rise above the transition issues that any church faces. An honest recognition of their various places in the life cycle and an attempt to be faithful to God have enabled all 32 to move boldly. The purpose of describing the life cycle is to make clear that a congregation can move into revitalization at *any* time in its life.

The congregational life cycle model used here has been more fully described in the book *Shaping the Coming Age of Religious Life.*[1] The research done by the authors of that study focused on religious orders of the Roman Catholic tradition. Most of these orders have had lifetimes numbering in hundreds of years. In the Western Hemisphere, a congregation's lifetime is obviously far shorter. A valid question is whether studies on religious orders spanning centuries can apply to congregations a few decades or a couple of centuries old. Let the model, as I have adapted it to congregational life, speak for itself. It includes five periods.

Foundation Period

The foundation period is the time when a congregation's life begins. "The first period in the life of a religious community centers around a founding person and his or her vision."[2] This "vision" can be a corporate one, as a congregation or a community of congregations aspires to begin a fresh community. Part of this new vision is a transforming experience, or moment, in which a "new appreciation" of the faith is caught. Following that experience by the founding person or community, a *new* community emerges. The first vision is shared, and it becomes the common property of the forming community. This community faces crises:

- Of *direction*, in which community members must decide which of their dreams and ideas can be achieved and which must be sacrificed.

- Of *leadership*, when decisions must be made about who will lead beyond the founder(s)/dreamer(s).

- Of *legitimization*, or in congregational terms, "Will this community receive ongoing church approval and support?"

The excitement and joy of the foundation (or formative period) can be deflated by expectations from internal or external sources that will require the community to grow up too fast. I have seen new congregations struggling early in their lives with such matters as finding land and erecting buildings while having no time to build a community of faith able to make decisions and withstand pressures.

Ideally, formation is not a time to worry, but a time to put dreams into action. Many of the people attracted to the formation of a religious community are pioneers in spirit, people who want to join one another and God in doing a new thing, people who would likely back away from a well-established congregation where norms and rules were already spelled out. Not too many people fit this profile, but when a community comes together to begin a new corporate life guided by God's spirit, theirs can be an exciting adventure.

In the contemporary religious world, in my view, every new parish or congregation goes through this initial period. But whereas the great orders of the church, such as the Franciscans and Benedictines, could take decades or centuries to undergo "foundation/formation," this re-freshing, grace-filled time has become shorter and shorter for contem-porary congregations. In fact, during the years when Americans of European ancestry were expanding their presence in North America and great numbers of congregations were being formed as part of the west-ward movement, this time of being established often lasted for decades. New congregations no longer have decades to be formed and established. Quite often, expectations demand that buildings, staffs, programs, and projects become more important than the dreams that gave birth to these faith ventures.

On three occasions I have been called in to help resolve conflicts in congregations ten years old. The issues faced were much like those faced by churches that were 50, 100, or 200 years old. In all three situ-ations a primary element in the conflict was that church members had been so drawn into filling expectations such as buying land, erecting a building, hiring a staff, and funding the budget that they had not formed deeply faithful communities along the way. They had not had time to do so. All three congregations had their own places of worship, the credi-bility of established congregations, and very fragile fellowships. They had been rushed, mostly by denominational expectations, to the expan-sion stage before it was time. The formation time should be long enough to allow a community to become sufficiently rooted and grounded in faith that even major traumas will be manageable.

Expansion Period

Emerging from the foundation period, the community "undergoes a fairly long period of expansion, during which the founding charism is institutionalized in a variety of ways."[3] During this time the founding myths are brought together into a belief system and structure that tries to make sense of life for the whole body, the church.

It is a time characterized by growth, particularly in numbers. One opinion holds that most Protestant congregations reach their "size" and character at the end of this period. They achieve an equilibrium of numbers and output that is comfortable and that will last into the indefinite future. Roman Catholic parishes differ from Protestant ones in that they purport to serve a defined geographical area, and the number of Catholic participants in that area may vary as time passes. But even in Catholic parishes, during the expansion period the parish's boundaries and space are defined.

In all cases, if the stages of growth and expansion are interrupted, the congregation may be jolted back to a new period of formation and foundation. Only the most devastating event—a natural disaster, a fire, some massive trauma—is likely to cause such a move backward during the expansion stage. While later stages may be more vulnerable, expansion is a hearty time of flexing muscles and believing that nothing can bring defeat.

Expansion is a time when practice and polity are tested and set in place. Community procedures are selected. Communication modes are practiced and blessed. New ways of reaching out are adopted, and members become excited because these enhance even broader recruitment possibilities.

It is important during the expansion time that the dreams and dreamers are still recognized. This is a time when the congregation needs to be reminded of its meaning and purpose. There is too much work to be done here to lay foundations of meaning again, as these will have been laid during "foundation-formation."

Quite often during this period organizational crises will confront the community, but these are unlikely to cause the congregation to move back to formation. Authority, methods of decisionmaking, strategies to integrate new members, ways of dealing with differences—these are but some of the organizational matters that can become major crises. It goes without saying that quality of community life, faith practices, and definitions of purpose need to have been established before such crises are encountered, or they can tear the community's thin fabric to shreds.

Stabilization Period

The stablilization period normally includes a sense of success, and members ordinarily derive a "high degree of personal satisfaction"[4] from just being in the community. To use marriage and family as an analogy, this is the time when children, having been born during "expansion," now grow up, get an education, and become established in life.

The congregation's purpose has been established, and the order of life is not to improve on that purpose but to carry it out. Often a sense prevails that life has always been the way it is, that it will remain so, and that there is no reason to change.

Quite often founders are no longer present. Those who embodied the dream, offering great energy and leadership in earlier times, are gone, and so the dream is but a memory. One would hope that the formation of a genuine Christian community would never be simply a "memory," but that the reason for this particular community's being could now be celebrated as more than a story out of the past, perhaps questioned at times, but not substantially changed.

Members can often "be simply carried along by the momentum of the community's activity."[5] They stay in the stabilization period because of expectations from within and from external forces such as the denomination.

Crises come during this time. Even logical and understandable suggestions for change may be rejected because they deviate from the pattern of the past. "We've always done it this way" can become a mantra that spells trouble for the next, or "breakdown" period. A crucial test of the congregation's viability becomes its capacity to adapt to new situations. Quite often it will find adaptability hard to deal with; life is dominated by powerful assumptions about doing things the same ways.

This can be a fruitful time. People who join the congregation during stabilization are often those who like a proven product, who are less adventurous than the pioneers who came earlier. This is a time when the task is to communicate solidity, predictability, and normality to members and friends.

A peril of this time: Satisfaction with the ways Christ's message has been interpreted may settle over the community. Vision and intensity can become victims of satisfaction. While productivity may be high, the seeds of future difficulty are planted by the satisfaction that drives much of the community's life.

Breakdown Period

This is a time of "dismantling of the institutional structures and belief systems that arose in the expansion period and served the community so well during the stabilization period."[6]

This period begins as some members become dissatisfied. They may see that the congregation works in a way that does not allow it to address certain problems. The "we've always done it this way" refrain is tested by people who ask "Why?"

Stress from several directions can increase. Groups may compete over how things are done. Doubts lead some to wonder if much can be accomplished. The congregation encounters new challenges. Procedures and structures designed to handle past pressures prove inadequate for the new time.

Distance from the dream and the dreamers of the foundation/formation period is a factor. In most institutions these periods are separated by more than one generation, so if some do remember the foundational vision, they may be too old to make much of a contribution. This distance makes most active participants less invested in the dream than were those on whose shoulders they stand. This distance prompts some to wonder what brought the congregation into being.

The question "What are we doing here?" can be addressed constructively, with the congregation seeking faithfully together for a fresh answer and purpose, or it can become a cynical and negative force leading some to wonder if there is any good reason for life in this church. If the question is addressed in a hopeful way, revitalization can follow.

On the other hand, if the congregation loses its sense of identity and purpose, service becomes "more haphazard and lacks direction."[7] Moral norms may become relaxed, and some members may distract themselves with ethical misconduct. At the same time there may be a loss of numbers, as members withdraw and recruitment of new people becomes more difficult. Polarization, demoralization, lack of focus, loss of energy—all are crises the congregation faces during this period. The plaguing question remains: What do we do as we disintegrate? Even more disturbing can be the tendency of some to ignore the realities of their life together, choosing instead to "list inexorably"[8] into lifelessness.

Critical Period

During this period "three outcomes are possible for the community: extinction, minimal survival, or revitalization."[9] For congregations this can mean death by indecision, death by choice, or revitalization.

To die by indecision is simply to fail to recognize the crisis, choosing to do business as usual, regardless of the consequences. As the 20th century ends, more Protestant congregations in the critical period are taking this course than any other. For many, perhaps, the options haven't become apparent. They may sense that something isn't right and yet not know what can be done. Other choices become moot, and the congregation simply loses life a bit at a time. Indeed, most congregations taking this course did not choose to slide into oblivion.Yet some have heard and seen the signs, viewed the alternatives, and chosen this course anyway. Because most American Protestant congregations have been around long enough to be in either the breakdown or critical period, one must wonder what the face of Protestantism will show 50 years hence.

Death by choice is the second option. A growing number of congregations recognize that they will not likely become revitalized, but they refuse to go down without committing their resources to the future of the church. And so such tools as reversionary clauses are used, in which the congregation chooses how to dispose of its resources if it ceases to exist as a viable congregation of its tradition. Some congregations, seeing that further ministry is impossible, decide to close and turn over their material assets to other organizations for continued ministry in fresh ways and places. A frequently chosen disposition of property enables the establishment of new congregations. Many denominations have resources to assist congregations facing such decisions.

Revitalization is the desired choice of some, but not many are able to experience it. Genuine revitalization calls for essentially dismantling the structures and assumptions that have guided the congregation. A renewal of faith, new appropriation of prayer and other spiritual disci-plines, and a fresh vision about the identity of this community are essential.

Revitalization will begin a new foundation/formation time. A whole new dream and fresh dreamers will emerge and, empowered by a rich sense of God's presence and guidance, will press the congregation to a new period of formation.

While it is early in our experience to make a conclusive judgment, it is likely that the life cycle will not last as long after a revitalizing time as it did the first time around. I say it is early because not enough American churches have undergone revitalization and lived far enough into the process for us to know how long a second life cycle might take. Because revitalization is one of the growing edges of religious life, we can learn about it only as we live it. If my own denomination is typical, and I suspect it is, it will be 30 to 40 years before the second life cycle's duration will be observable.

There is good reason to believe that life cycles of religious congre-gations are becoming shorter, even as the life cycle of the individual person is lengthening. This is a curious reality of our time. Probably because of "future shock," as discussed earlier, in which the future seems to come at us much more rapidly than ever, we learn more quickly, forget faster, change focus more often, and are more easily distracted. Thus change becomes a stronger force than ever in congregational life.

It is important to recall that no period is any better than any other, that every congregation is at some point in this cycle, and that our call is to seek the will of God at whatever point we find ourselves. The adage "bloom where you are planted" must guide us as we try to discern what God desires in our congregation's next steps.

Study Congregations and the Life Cycle

The 32 congregations whose pastorates I studied represent a range of points on the life cycle. I intentionally sought congregations that had been at different positions in the life cycle when they began to experi-ence vitality.

Eight congregations were in the foundation/formation or expan-sion period. These include a group of 30 young Asian Americans in

Baltimore who had been meeting for only a few months; two booming 12-year-old congregations, each with at least 800 members and growing almost daily; and three that started, stuttered, and, after seeking new, energetic builder-pastors, began rapid growth.

Ten congregations are in the stabilization period and are healthy and productive communities. Common to many was a sense that things were starting to level out, life was not as exciting as it had been, and the first hints of breakdown were showing themselves. All of them recommitted themselves to dramatic and faithful life together, and are experiencing a new expansion time.

Fourteen pastors described their congregations as deep in the critical period when they arrived. Without giving themselves kudos of any kind, these pastors told stories of typical congregations that had been around long enough to be near death without knowing it, and which, by God's grace, were led to life in part because of an amazing marriage (my words) of pastor and people. Not all believed their congregations had fully emerged from the critical time. But all these congregations had at minimum begun to face the meaning of this period. Two congregations had previously had pastorates of over 40 years. In one, a disaster hit shortly after the new, young pastor's arrival, offering a time to seal his role and authority as pastor. In the other, no such event occurred, and the pastor has had to work patiently, faithfully, to see life slowly change as people made decisions and commitments of resources they feared to make earlier in her pastorate there.

There is no magic time when revitalization takes hold. Hard work, spiritual disciplines, endless listening, the faith that God is present with the people through all sorts of risks, and earning the members' trust because they know the pastor will stay with them through the long haul— all are elements in revitalizing pastorates. Many of us can take strength and encouragement from their example. Devoted pastoral leadership is necesssarily a primary element in the revitalization of a dying congregation.

A Four-Faceted Understanding of Congregational Growth

What does growth mean for congregations? Some hold that a congregation is not viable with fewer than 600 members. Others contend that small is the magic word, that the church should be a place where everybody knows your name. "Growth" has for many become not just a goal, but a hammer, a goad, a magic wand, and when narrowly understood, a way of separating congregational sheep from goats. That is to say, congregations that aren't adding members at a pace that outstrips their losses are too often considered deficient. And so this word "growth" has taken on a singular meaning that is unfair to congregations and unfaithful to God.

We are looking at growth because the prototype approach holds that while change is inevitable, we need to strive for change that will be congruent with Ephesians 4:15, to "grow up in every way into Christ." Congregations will always undergo life-cycle transitions. These happen. But the ways they happen can seem to be good or bad. As they are happening, is it not our responsibility to work for good changes and directions in the congregation's life? This model of growth is one way of understanding change.

This four-dimensional understanding has its roots in a Scripture text familiar to many: "And Jesus grew in wisdom, and in years, and in divine and human favor" (Luke 2:52, NRSV). I apply these words about Jesus' own growth and development to describe the congregation—to represent *stewardship*, *evangelism*, *spirituality*, and *compassion*. This verse is one of a few that describe Jesus' growth to adulthood, and offers a model of growth for the congregation.

Put simply, if our call is to imitate Jesus, then is not the growth of our gathered faith communities, our congregations, one facet of that imitation? I know that this effort has helped plain-spoken people in sincere congregations focus their life and aim it in constructive directions.

What's important to know about the four-dimensional "window" on a congregation's life is this: if none of these modes of growth is happening, the congregation is in difficulty, wherever it is located in the life cycle. And if only one form of growth is occurring, with no effort to develop others, the result is a "cancer of the church," in which the energy committed to one growth mode absorbs all other life in the congregation, and everything is focused on doing a single thing. An obvious example is Holy Name in chapter one, a congregation that has great evangelism and numerical growth with no spiritual or other growth dimensions to give meaning to them.

All of the pastors surveyed were asked to look at their lives through this lens.

Wisdom Means Stewardship

In many passages in Hebrew Scriptures, people who want to be loyal to God, individually or in community, are called to give wise oversight to God's creation. "Then God said, 'Let us make humankind in our image, according to our likeness and let them have dominion over . . . [everything]'" (Gen. 1:26). Stewardship is about caring for everything that God has created. "The metaphor of the steward comes into its own when Christians grasp that it is *the world* that they are called by grace to serve and to 'keep.'"[10]

For the congregation struggling to perpetuate its program or just to stay alive, stewardship may quickly come to refer only to money. But in this rich biblical sense, stewardship is concerned with all we do in managing the resources God has placed in our trust. Faithful stewardship celebrates the good news that God trusts the people. It is sometimes difficult, amazing, virtually unbelievable to absorb the truth that God trusts us. Stewardship is acknowledging God's trust and acting as God's servants.

One pastor said the most significant stewardship issue to be faced is how to manage time. Living in a generally affluent community, the members find time more precious than money. From this example, we can understand that stewardship means more than only money.

Another pastor related that the congregation's most exciting development, after a pastorate of many changeless (or so it seemed) years, was that "we are learning to release the hold on resources," meaning in particular space, but time and money also.

Stewardship, then, is about what we do with money, time, talents, space, nature, and all the other treasures we have.

In 80 percent of the congregations interviewed, stories of growth in stewardship were told. Most exciting were the stories of those who said they were in the critical period and that new growth and hope described their stewardship life. Just as hopeful were the young congregations that had early established faithful stewardship of life as an important part of their characters.

Congregations in the stabilization period tended to report less growth and change in stewardship, but even so, several indicated that renewal and the resulting change had sparked stewardship growth. In these, new stewardship energies were coming most often from a fresh devotion to a focus of mission and ministry in the community. One congregation, long established in its city, had placed great emphasis on housing as its "major" work, and attracted people with that interest. Decisions about money, space construction and use, time, and program were aimed at providing housing.

Stature means Evangelism

I regard evangelism as entailing far more than how many people join a congregation. Rooted in the word *evangel*, which means "good news," evangelism is about the extent to which the good news, the gospel of the church, reaches and touches people's lives. Does it make a difference to people? What kind of difference? Is it a difference that could be made no other way?

Surprisingly, most of the pastors said that they did not have pre-designed evangelism programs. Rather, they sought to place emphasis on the degree to which members related their own faith experience to others. One pastor said his congregation's is a "go to, rather than a come to, evangelism." People are encouraged to witness, not by beating people over the head with their message, but simply by sharing the meaning of their own faith life.

Not one congregation stated that programs specially designed to bring in new members had been successful. Some had tried; none had produced. The general tenor of comments indicated that when evangelism is crammed into a programmatic emphasis, it won't work. The evangel is more a description of the congregation's character and energy than of particular programs and strategies.

In congregations that have gained the most new members, it is clear that at some point momentum became a factor, and people simply began

coming. Seldom did they come because of the reputation of the preacher. Sometimes the congregation's emphases drew them. Most of these
new people came because someone invited them. This momentum has a
spontaneous quality, best defined as that time when members so value
their life together and its spiritual meaning that they are eager to invite
others. This eagerness contrasts sharply with the oft-discussed reluctance
of many people in this culture even to name their faith and church, lest
they be belittled, even scorned.

In some situations a major appeal to new people was based on the
unique character of the congregation. This was most often true in niche
churches, where a special ministry was the dominant motif. The church
with a particular emphasis on housing has a strong attraction to people
who care about housing as a matter of faith and public policy. As a
result, many have been drawn there and have become members. Of
course, that church didn't take on housing to attract new people but
because members heard this venture as God's call. And certainly many
people hear about the housing ministry from members. Newcomers experience that call to ministry as an authenticating factor of their church's
mission and character.

The congregations varied widely in numbers, from several dozen in
the new Asian-American community to over 8,000 in a large, historically
African-American urban church. The average number of participating
members at the beginnings of the current pastors' ministries was 312.
Net additions to membership were 927. Their current participating
membership averages 1,239. More important are the differences between the congregations in character, mission, and length of the pastors'
tenures. However, to the degree that 20 of the 32 indicated sufficient
growth to call for changes in the ways their congregations lead their
lives, and that all of these report significant teaching programs as a part
of new-member entry or assimilation, this growth can be seen as lasting,
faith-changing evangelism.

The teaching programs are a significant part of the congregations'
lives. From a four-session class on "developing a personal relationship
with Jesus Christ" to year-long seminary level Bible and theology
classes for adults, these congregations take teaching seriously. Teaching
will be discussed in more detail in the next growth area, but we need to
see it as integral to evangelism. Parishes offer entry classes or membership classes, and in most of the churches, entering or newly received

members are either required, seriously encouraged, or persuasively invited to take part in such training.

Favor with God Means Spirituality

Earlier I shared McLaughlin's definition of spirituality as the degree to which the word we hear from God influences and changes the decisions we make and thus the way we live. Spirituality is not a separate world, apart from everyday struggles and joys.

I wanted to find out the extent to which these congregations work with purpose to offer people ways to hear God and then to reflect on what this voice is saying. Certainly neither the congregation nor the pastor can always determine if that heard word results in changes, though sometimes the effects will be obvious. But both clergy and laity can enhance the opportunities available to people to hear the word, and be present as people struggle to apply that word to their living.

Eighty percent described significant ways of helping people encounter God's voice. All agreed that God not only speaks to them—that indeed, God can choose to speak in any way. But there are ways and means whereby the church can help people experience God's presence. They include teaching, worship, prayer groups, group encounter, counseling, and servant ministries.

Worship was particularly important to many of the pastors:

- "Seeker worship is emphasized."
- "Worship is deliberately joyful, with contemporary music."
- "Worship is intentionally one-third contemporary, one-third classical, and one-third Gospel. People like the blend."
- "There is a sense that God is alive in the church, in worship."
- "Spirituality is teaching the ground of being."
- "Worship is vital, inclusive of several cultures."

Worship for many is the event in which the congregation is offered up to God. It is almost as though a mirror of the people is held up and given to God each time they gather.

By and large, these are not theologically conservative congregations, though they include a far wider range than the traditional mainline.

Still, as activist as many are, it is encouraging to know that such activism is coupled with a life of spiritual devotion. On the face of it, this makes sense, because the faith community needs nurture to be able to serve. Many congregations have burned out in active doing of the word, without sufficient listening and hearing to feed them. But these congregations are different. One pastor spoke for many when he said, "Understanding God is basic for everyone who comes in." Several described deliberate work by groups such as elders to know, in another pastor's words, "the mind of Christ" for their individual lives and their life together. Important to a number is the relation of spirituality to stewardship —as though the two words were interchangeable.

Bible study is a core activity for nearly all the congregations. Not only the studies described earlier for new entrants but also continuing mission-focused studies are common. In one old and recovering urban church, more and more people are becoming engaged in Bible study that focuses on stewardship, public witness, and dealing with interpersonal differences. A revitalized church used home Bible studies for several years, and these became important entry points for new people into the church. In a young and growing church, Bible study is "at the center of every event."

Several pastors told how important preaching is to the Bible study programs, with a handful using preaching texts for lay study groups. "Truth-telling" is a phrase some pastors use to describe their approach to preaching, with less emphasis placed on a problem-centered theme and more on an exegetical style.

Most pastors told of active involvement of their members in experiences ranging from prayer partnerships to retreats. By coincidence, I spoke with two pastors of largely African-American congregations at times when they had just called on their congregations to engage in fasting and prayer for particular concerns. The picture of hundreds of people taking part in this kind of discipline simultaneously, in congregations often vitally engaged in community outreach ministries, is new to many. Nearly all pastors said that the congregations both trusted and expected them as pastors to call people to prayer and spiritual direction. One said, "This is at the heart of who I am and what I do."

Favor with Humans Means Compassion

Life in God's way is "a gift not to possess but to share."[11] Henri Nouwen describes our world "of strangers, estranged from their own past, culture and country, from their neighbors, friends and family, from their deepest self and their God" as one where "we witness a painful search for a hospitable place where life can be lived without fear and where community can be found."[12]

The congregation's quality of life is often seen in the degree to which there is a passion for community, the unlovely are at home, and people are willing to care for the disenfranchised who normally are not to be found within the walls of a church.

None of the pastors was ready to say that the work of the congregation can easily make major changes in the fabric of society that keeps people in harsh places. Indeed, several pastors said their primary emphasis is to empower people to serve where they are in the world, rather than to establish programs and places for service by members.

The African-American congregations take very seriously the congregation's responsibility to confront the corporate evils of the world. They hold that racism lies behind much of this evil. Two historic congregations in Baltimore are places where such notable anti-racism battle groups as the NAACP and before that the Niagara Movement took root. Many have long been committed to activities that confront economic and political forces that discriminate (like the garbage workers' strike in Memphis, 1968). Even more do active work to eliminate the scourge of homelessness. These congregations are on the front lines of servant ministry.

Examples of compassionate outreach were plentiful. One pastor called for other congregations in Washington, D.C. to join his church in adopting gangs so these young people could experience hospitality rather than hostility from institutions in the District of Columbia. Another cited ecumenical efforts through the county's community ministry program, which addresses homelessness, shut-in isolation, housing discrimination, and educational discrimination. Several identified national projects such as refugee resettlement, Habitat for Humanity (which is local *and* national), and denominational mission activities as ways to share their gifts with others.

Sixty-five percent of the pastors spoke of their congregations' involvement in hands-on outreach efforts. This number goes beyond those who only urge their people to do the truth in their daily lives. The efforts are encouraging because they are not being undertaken just to make the doers feel good, but because they are the right thing to do. One pastor observed: "We are working on the sacred truth: all are one. Your pain is mine, your joy my joy. We are not satisfied with the way we live together on this earth . . . what one person does makes a difference."

Study Congregations

All 32 pastors interviewed found this way of looking at growth to be an important model for reflecting on their congregations' lives. This model describes four ways of growing, and each pastor named at least two of the four as happening in his or her congregation. Two-thirds named three. A handful described growth in all four modes.

The Church of Tomorrow

Once while traveling in a group of college students en route to a national conference, I visited a church of my denomination that had just built a futuristic structure. Such construction might not seem so unusual today. It comprised three buildings—a geodesic dome, an education space, and a needlelike tower encircled by a wall, an artistic construct over which stood the cross. The pastor proudly called it "the church of tomorrow." Whatever the physical structure, churches of tomorrow exhibit today's three qualities. They are (1) spiritual vitality, (2) a face to the world, and (3) spiritually gifted pastoral leadership. The first two will be described here. The third forms the core of the next chapter.

Every congregation seems to exist on a continuum between "maintenance" and "mission"—that is, between staying alive and giving itself away. These extremes have sometimes been described in bold, even unfair, terms. To be maintenance-bound means to care only about keeping the doors open, bringing in enough income to pay the bills, keeping the current members happy at all costs (because, after all, they pay the bills), and doing anything possible to survive. This might be called the congregational version of being self-obsessed. To be mission-driven means to give ourselves to others sacrificially, to take great risks for others, often giving up a sound budget, building maintenance, congregational community, and administrative concerns. It is as though these two extremes cannot co-exist. Either we are all wrapped up in ourselves, or we are oblivious to staying alive and we will die to do the caring thing.

Hear this: neither maintenance nor mission is a four-letter word! If maintenance means paying the bills, using the property wisely, and ensuring that parts don't wear out unnecessarily, then it is necessary. It is when these become the only business of the church that we are in trouble. If mission means caring compassionately for all of God's creation, then it is necessary. It is when this becomes the sole work of the church, with no source of support to sustain this giving-away process, that we are in trouble.

The maintenance-mission continuum appears to become a focus of conflict as a congregation moves into the "breakdown" and "critical" periods. Because so many congregations today are preoccupied with whether they will survive much longer, this tension is probably more aggravated than ever before.

In the face of this struggle to survive or die, we look at signs apparent in the vital congregation. In looking at the 32 pastorates, these signs were distinctive marks.

Spiritual Vitality

Again and again pastors told me that the congregations they serve are undergirded by a nourishing spiritual life. Just as a body needs to eat as well as exercise, so a church and its members must be fed with the food of God. This is more easily said than done. God's self-disclosure happens in more places than we can name, but it is the congregation's task to expose people to multiple ways of encountering the eternal.

These pastors told of congregations that have grown beyond a time when they thought they could survive by sheer human power. None spoke pejoratively of the recent past, in which many congregations became engaged in good works while brushing off suggestions that the people, individually and collectively, need to be nurtured to do these

good deeds. But they were clear, nonetheless, that Christians who care
about confronting evils like racism, sexism, poverty, and the abuse of
creation need to experience spiritually nurturing and sustaining activities.
Some go all out in their attacks on these evils with no thought of their
own welfare and sustenance. They pay a high price in deflation of spirit.

Without apology, these congregations work to equip participants for
ministry. Worship, Bible study, prayer, spiritual formation, quality
pastoral care, and counseling are offered up as ways of enabling people
to find the spiritual help they need to live lives of faith and devoted
service.

The church that is alive is a center of spiritual growth. Members
experience change in their relationships with God. These congregations
challenge people to engage in spirituality in ways that can result in
growth and change.

One of the first disciplines in which this change becomes evident is
stewardship. People grow as genuine stewards as they grow in their relationship to God and as that affects the decisions they make about how
to manage everything in their lives. It is fair to ask: Is my stewardship
today—be it money, time, skills, or whatever—the same as a year ago?
If I have not changed and expanded in what I do with these and other
gifts of God, then growth isn't taking place.

The evidence of spirituality is present elsewhere as well. *Koinonia*,
or partnership, between God and us and among us as members will become stronger. The liveliness of worship as the primary event in which
the congregation celebrates God's mighty acts will increase. The seri-
ousness with which the church, and we, take studying Scripture and
other faith-focused sources will deepen.

Suffice it to say that the vital, renewed, and renewing congregation
will be a place where people are offered opportunities to meet God and
grow.

A Face to the World

Too often devoted lay members as well as pastors have said, "As soon as
we get our internal life worked out and healthy, we will be able to reach
out and touch the world beyond us."

In the vital congregation, the Scripture's second law is an active fact: "You shall love your neighbor as yourself." That is to say, if we love only ourselves and try to get ourselves fixed, we will never complete the law. As with an individual, the self-absorbed congregation is not healthy. The mental health specialist will describe the person preoccupied with self as neurotic. Being self-absorbed may be the result of evil forces, but one who is self-absorbed cannot be dismissed simply as an evil person. There are causes of self-absorption, for individuals as well as for congregations.

The congregation that stays self-absorbed because it believes that financial and other problems must be dealt with first is a congregation that will not come alive. Fear of weakening and dying most often drives congregations into this posture. The record of congregations that have died by indecision will show that, by and large, they lost a sense of mission and ministry to the world beyond. It is a strange irony that the more obsessed a congregation becomes with its survival, the more self-destructive are its actions. Self-absorption can signal the congregation's death-knell.

Turning a face to the world is not, however, something that a congregation should do only to stay alive. Rather, caring about the world beyond ourselves, the world God is creating and continues to cherish, is our responsibility simply because it is God's desire for us.

This was a relentless point of faith for pastors. They voiced strong convictions that anything we share is multiplied many times over when this sharing is done with no expectation of a return. We reach out, they said, not because if we don't we'll die, but because it is what God beckons us to do.

The face to the world is a quality that defines both evangelism approaches and compassionate ministries. With no expectation of any institutional gain, one congregation conducts Bible study as part of its ministry with homeless people. Another offers a place safe from violence for kids in a tough neighborhood. Yet another combined creativity, compassion, and courage in establishing a care center for the babies of young women in the county who would otherwise be unable to complete high school. One of the highest risk examples is the congregation that invested millions of dollars to build not only an education unit, but a building that could be quickly converted from education space to a homeless shelter and back again.

When evangelism is carried out simply because God calls us to reach people with a word of meaning, hope, and life, and not because we are bent on recruiting members, then our efforts will be pleasing to God.

When the congregation stretches a healing hand to the dispossessed, not to make its members feel good but because this is the mandate of God, that action will be pleasing to the Almighty.

It is not easy work for a congregation to develop this paired sense of healthy maintenance and commitment to God's created order. Most congregations do not have these two elements in good balance. It is an appropriate lens through which all congregational life might well be viewed. Essential to a congregation's coming to hold these two in faithful and healthy tension is leadership. To that we turn next.

CHAPTER 5

Tomorrow's Shepherds

How beautiful upon the mountains
are the feet of the messenger who announces peace,
who brings good news.

(Isa. 52:7a)

It would be time-consuming to express fully our concerns about the
social disintegration, the moral disorientation, and the spinning
compass needle of our time. So we cry out for leadership.

—John Gardner[1]

Future church leadership will be "in but not of" the world and has a
quality different from that called for in the past. Transition is so rapid in
these times that we can hardly catch our breath as we seek to *see* that
change. The church needs leadership that is spiritually centered, trusted
and trusting, looking to a future of hope, mission-focused, committed to
shared leadership and truth-telling, and attuned to the world.

But first, what is leadership? Because God works in the whole world
as well as in the church, much can be learned from the larger world of
leadership.

Social systems cannot work for more than an instant without leadership. Someone will always have to step up and call others to move together in some direction. Whether it's a herd of horses, a pod of seals, a
team of oxen or of athletes, all will sit around and look at each other,
and look out for themselves, unless someone says, "Let's go there" or
"Let's stay here," "Let's do that" or "Let's not do this."

Leadership itself is value-neutral. "Leadership" does not imply a
particular value to the task at hand. Both Hitler and Churchill were

leaders. Nor does the word suggest that one leadership method is more important than others. Some think of military prowess when they think of leaders. Even in battle, some say a leader leads best by being in the midst of the action, while others maintain that leading works best from a lofty distance. But many would cite Martin Luther King, Jr., and Mother Teresa as two of the truly great leaders of this century, with their respective missions about as far from the battlefield as one can get.

Some Definitions

An abundance of literature has been produced in recent years about leadership—a fact that speaks to the great need for leadership and creative models for it.

What or who is a leader?

• *John Gardner:* "Leadership is the process of persuasion or example by which an individual [or leadership team] induces a group to pursue objectives held by the leader or shared by the leader and his or her followers." [2]

• *John Kotter:* "And those people at the top of enterprises today who encourage others to leap into the future, who help them overcome natural fears, and who thus expand the leadership capacity in their organizations—these people provide a profoundly important service for the entire human community."[3]

• *Margaret J. Wheatley:* "If we succeed in maintaining focus, rather than hands-on control, we also create the flexibility and responsiveness that every organization craves. What leaders are called upon to do in a chaotic world is to shape their organizations through concepts, not through elaborate rules or structures."[4]

From these and other definitions, my own experience as a leader, years of working with and observing leaders in the church, and conversations with many extraordinary pastor-leaders, comes this definition of tomorrow's pastor-leader: *The pastor-leader, tomorrow's shepherd,*

relying on God's power, presence, and guidance, will create a vision,
engender trust, communicate a firm sense of mission, and then act
with commitment to that mission. This leader will work with the con-
gregation, enabling its members to share and own this mission and be
drawn together into God's future.

Managing versus Leading

It is important to distinguish between managing and leading. Managers
give oversight to what is happening each hour and day. Leaders give
vision to what will happen in the days and years to come. Managers,
says John Kotter, do planning and budgeting, organizing and staffing,
controlling and problem-solving. Leaders establish direction, align,
motivate, and inspire people. Managers produce a degree of predictability; leaders produce change.[5] Both are necessary. Perish the organization that relies only on vision, with no capacity to manage what comes
of its dreaming. And similarly, how stale the organization that knows
how to organize and manage but has no driving sense of direction. It
would be naive, even stupid, to assume that church pastors are *either*
leaders or managers. Most congregations don't have the luxury of calling both, even if they could find them! As a result, many ministers will
be leader-managers, having to draw together the two tasks into one vocational style, and evoking these respective gifts in lay leaders, their
daily partners in ministry.
    When we understand the difference between leader and manager,
and the importance of both in the pastor's role, and add the critical
element of spiritual direction, then we can begin to see a picture of the
future pastor-leader.

Leadership and Change

I asked pastors about their role as change agents. Because change is not
always democratic, and just to be alive is to change, I was looking, more
particularly, for an understanding of how change can move in God's
direction with faith, hope, and love.

I wanted to know what kind of leader can guide such change. One way of understanding the charismatic leader is to see this person as a primary change agent. "Historically we find that charismatic leaders have always personified the forces of change, unconventionality, vision..."[6] Jay Conger goes on to assert that "charismatic leaders are tireless challengers of the status quo—relentless in their search for new approaches. [Because of their gifts], charismatic leaders are potential sources of enormous transformation."[7]

Change happens. But it need not *just* happen. If congregational change is to happen in God's direction, then committed and challenging pastor-leaders are called for.

I asked the pastor-leaders five questions that gave us information about their leadership:

- Are you trusted to tell the truth and take the consequences? How?
- Are you trusted to lead in fresh directions and call the people to follow? How?
- Are you trusted to be a reconciler in an "in-your-face" culture? How?
- Are you trusted to be the one who calls the people to spiritual growth? How?
- Describe your leadership style as best you can in this framework: telling, selling, facilitating, collaborating.

Seven qualities of leadership became clear as we talked. Though the pastors were not asked specifically about these seven qualities, they are presented in rank-order of importance based on the pastors' comments. None of the 32 pastors would claim all seven as his or her gifts. All would say, however, that being spiritually grounded and being free to trust and be trusted are vital. Nearly all would agree, further, that being visionary and mission-focused is necessary. The majority identified a "collaborative" leadership style as best for them, yet also lifted up "telling," as in truth-telling, as a core leadership practice. Finally, most stressed the importance of being culturally attuned.

Their words, with commentary on each of the seven qualities in the order of importance, follow. As I examine the emerging shepherd, the future pastor, I will compare the emerging role with past role expectations of pastors.

The Spiritually Grounded Pastor

One pastor said, "This [being spiritually grounded] is at the heart of who I am."

Grounded is a synonym for "anchored," "rooted," or "planted." I choose "grounded" because it has several meanings, all of which recognize that the ground is under everything. Foundations rest in the ground. Currents, whether electrical or water, are undergirded by the ground. Life grows from the ground, and remains always connected to the ground. To ground someone in a field of inquiry is to help them learn the most basic information about it. To be spiritually grounded means to be so dependent on the spirit of God that you go back again and again for insight, inspiration, strength, and rest, and you can't do anything in your ministry without these.

One pastor prays for hours early every morning. "I seek the mind of Christ. God and I spend a lot of time together." Others observe regular times of fasting and prayer. "They see me listening to God. They know I practice spiritual disciplines."

One called herself a practitioner of "realistic mysticism." Another said, "I have a rest-and-do cycle in my life," with "rest" being times to pray, listen, and "drink in" the spirit of God, and "do" being the times to act. Neither can exist without the other.

Not all of the pastors practice spiritual disciplines in the same ways. Notable are several whose spirituality is most often a shared experience. "I pray with everyone." Another told me that he has "prayed with at least 85 to 90 percent of the people in the parish," and it is no small congregation.

A common theme to their spirituality was voiced by one who said, "I don't ask them [parishioners] to do what I won't do." Now, this wisdom could be applied to every dimension of faithful leadership, because, like Jesus himself, a leader needs to be willing to do whatever she or he asks others to do. But these pastor-leaders take seriously the reality that people look to their actions more than their words for learning. Vital to their integrity is the fact that they do not call on people to pray, meditate, study the Scripture, listen for God's voice, and then go off and ignore these disciplines themselves. Integrity is a vital part of being spiritually grounded.

To do what they say they will do is crucial to these pastors. One pastor said, "They think I'm braver than I am." This pastor's "bravery" is not measured by glossy deeds of heroism but by the fact that he struggles, often openly, with difficult decisions, living honestly in the midst of life's ambiguities, and he almost always emerges with a heartfelt, thought-out strategy that the people trust. This trust is based more on the way he grapples with such issues than on the outcome. Even when people disagree with his conclusion, they have a deep respect for the integrity of his struggle. This, for the congregation, is a core part of spirituality: they see him making decisions in the light of what he believes God wants.

There is another side to the pastor's spirituality, for being a spiritual person seems to give the pastor-leaders the secure place from which to be transparent about their own vulnerabilities. "I am open about my mistakes, and they are willing to follow because of this." This kind of openness also helps define the pastor-leader's role, or the perception the laity have of that role: "We don't want you to be our savior (i.e., be perfect) but just to work with us." The pastors hold that if they are candid in and about their conversations with God and increasingly secure in the grace of God, then they have no reason not to be clear and honest with the people in the congregation.

Often the people seek spiritual guidance from their pastors. "People have asked me to be their spiritual director." It is intriguing to see social-activist pastors also being spiritual directors. A few years ago this would have been an unheard-of combination. In fact, much of the moderate-liberal religious world saw these two roles as virtually incompatible. But this view is changing rapidly as energetic, mission-focused pastors discover that they cannot do the work of mission unless their own spirits are nourished. This does not mean that they compromise principles of justice and truth but that they become powerfully aware of what gives them the fuel to be principled pastors.

When pastors are seen practicing spiritual disciplines, they are often asked to share these practices. More and more pastors, many of the activists whose voices are heard here, are under spiritual direction and are learning to be effective spiritual directors.

More laity are asking these days not just for spiritual answers but for guidance in seeking these answers. This trend casts the pastor in a far healthier light than resident holy person. For some, this latter tired perception will hang around, but for a growing number the pastor is becoming a teacher of disciplines rather than a fount of all truth who can be blamed for giving poor advice.

It cannot be stated too often that spiritual growth in the congregation will not take place if the pastor is not spiritually grounded. Willing to be surprised and changed by God's voice, the emerging pastor-leader will not shun the watchful eyes of congregants who see in this person a believable spirituality. Nor can it be stated too often that the pastor doesn't practice the spiritual disciplines just to become more believable. That charade would become transparent. The pastor's spiritual grounding begins with his or her need.

Clearly the pastor's role is changing rapidly in the area of spirituality. In the recent past, public and priestly functions were the primary spiritual roles expected of the pastor. Today those functions may be shared with lay leaders and, though they remain important for the pastor, personal spirituality is emerging as a critical and visible part of the pastor's leadership. There is a growing openness to this role in many congregations, for though we know that Jesus said to pray privately, literally "in your closet," to avoid making a display of piety, this new spirituality seems not to be piety as much as necessity. It is becoming one of the pastor's most important personal resources *and* forms of witness.

The Trusted and Trusting Pastor

"Our present national culture—social, economic, even artistic, as well as political—is inhospitable to trust."[8] These words of sociologist Jack Gibb from 20 years ago are even truer today. In contrast, the vital and spiritually nourished church will be a place where trust thrives.

Healthy trust is not an uninformed, blind yielding. Gibb goes on to say that "wherever people are close and intimate, loving, interdependent and open to one another; wherever instinct or knowledge gives us a sense of being able to be ourselves with others, that provides a basis for trust."[9]

Trust comes from the German word *trost*, meaning *comfort.*[10] When I trust, I am confident I can be at ease with the person I trust. The pastors named the capacities to trust and be trusted as of equal importance to spiritual grounding in the effectiveness of their vocations. They said things like:

• "I'm here for a while, for the long haul. They know this and it gives them confidence."

- "They trust me to be there to suffer with them."
- "If you run, they won't trust you."

These reflections point to the importance of high-quality long tenure as a means of gaining trust. Nearly two decades ago an Alban Institute study of long pastorates identified two types of trust. In a pastorate of ten years or longer, barring unanticipated problems, *personal* trust between pastor and individual congregants would always increase. At the same time, *corporate* trust, that of pastor and "the people" for each other, would become strained, often lessened, as programs, practices, and messages were repeated and people came to take each other for granted. The resulting gap in the two kinds of trust—personal and corporate—must be monitored regularly so it does not widen and become destructive.[11]

Because of the different lengths of these pastorates (from three months to 35 years), if tenure were the only way to measure trust, the depth of trust would vary widely. But an added view of trust emerges. In all of these pastorates at least two of the modes of growth described in chapter four (stewardship, evangelism, spirituality, and compassion) occur. When the pastorate is vital, it is likely that personal and corporate trust are present and well managed, whatever the tenure. This is an important reason for the congregation's vitality. Further, the congregation is not so self-preoccupied that inordinate amounts of energy are placed on whether pastor and people get along.

In this context we can begin to see the power of trust that comes when people know that the pastor is "here for the long haul. I won't just cut and run." Trust grows to this level in part because the laypeople have made informed decisions about their trust of the pastor. A note of caution is advised, though, because such trust can become blind. So while many of the pastors spoke of the high degree of trust shared with parishioners, beware that such trust doesn't become a nest full of warm fuzzies that blinds the trusting ones to problems that come with being comfortable with each other. The pastors gave support to informed trust:

- "They defer to the track record."
- "Trust has been earned."
- "They trust me because I am not afraid of conflict."
- "They have been able to count on me."

These words were not uttered in a spirit of self-congratulation. No arms were broken by pastors patting themselves on the back. They were simply speaking the truth about their relationships with members. It might have sounded self-aggrandizing if only one or two rather than the majority had said such things. At first hearing, there seemed a touch of swagger in their comments, until the tones and moods, the accompanying comments and the deep spirituality, were heard as well. These comments about earned trust speak well of the pastors' self-confidence. It would be difficult to look at the record of gains, initiatives undertaken, and difficulties overcome, without expecting these clergy to grow in self-confidence. To be able to see what has happened during one's time as pastor, to know that one's leadership has played a real part in this change, and at the same time to continue to insist that God had the most to do with it, is what marks this special pastor-leader. No wonder people trust such pastors!

Unique to the issue of trust is the role of the pastor in the African-American church. "In the African-American church, corporate trust is forced on the pastor," one pastor commented. This was said with both a sense of reality and an almost plaintive wish that it weren't so. In that same Alban Institute study of long pastorates we learned that when a pastor first comes to a church, corporate trust accompanies the office. As personal trust builds, by the pastor's being with individuals and families through life crises, and the people come to know the pastor, corporate trust diminishes. No African-American pastorates were included in the study. Had there been, we may have found a different picture, one where corporate trust continues to run high throughout a pastorate, and the two types of trust grow on virtually parallel tracks. This may well contribute to understanding the visible community role and responsibility that African-American pastors appear to have, as well as the significant growth that has taken place in many historically African-American congregations. This level of responsibility can be a tough expectation to live with, but it is also one that has resulted in powerful ministries.

Pastors also spoke of how, in this trusting environment, members perceived them:

- "I am a non-anxious presence."
- "They see my willingness to listen and learn, and to value frank talking."

*   "They don't trust a minister who wants to overpower the
    congregation."

Patience, a manner that reflects genuine respect for others, combined
with such skills as active listening, clear speaking, and a capacity to
make sense of and use feedback effectively, all add to the trust people
feel for these pastors. I once heard an unpopular pastor described as a
person who was always looking over your shoulder while shaking your
hand, as though the next person in line was more important than you.

The clear truth is that effective pastors really enjoy people. They
don't just act the part. More than ever before, it is vital for pastors to
help others realize how important they are. This need for affirmation
seems to grow as technology depersonalizes much of life. The church is
a countercultural entity, prophetically different in times that call for
conformity. Encouraging spiritual dependence on God in a world where
false self-sufficiency is in vogue, the church becomes increasingly personal as technology makes much of life less personal. This climate can
create stress, because the pastor's inclination may be, for example, to do
a lot of touching, in an era when even a well-meant hug can lead to a
lawsuit.

Concern and care for others is the critical element. Pastors who
don't want to be around people don't last. An early Alban Institute study
found that many pastors who are involuntarily terminated ("fired" in
plain talk) were perceived, among other things, as not liking the laity.[12]
I once heard a school official describe a brilliant young principal of a
new school as knowing everything there was to know about education
and administration, but "he just doesn't like to have his school cluttered
up with kids."

If a person doesn't like people, how can he or she make it in the
congregational pastorate? Such a person ought to seek another way to
serve God. On the other hand, do not confuse a dislike of people with
introversion. Just as surely as an extrovert may be perceived as obnox-
iously noisy and intrusive because of a disinclination to be alone and
silent, so an introvert—who may be perceived as withdrawn, even shy—
can truly care about and want to be with others for fruitful and reward-
ing interactions.

One of the most refreshing parts of my conversations with the pastor-
leaders was hearing their excitement as they spoke of parishioners. They

really do like being with them, listening, understanding, even challenging and being challenged by them. What is just as clear is that their congregations know and respect this affection in their pastors. The pastors said:

- "I am trusted because I trust."
- "People pick it up if you are trustable."
- "I have not formed alliances."
- "They [feel that] they have been able to count on me."

Trustability, the pastors told me, is a result both of being known as reliable *and* being willing to trust others. None of these pastors acted as though the people were insignificant and didn't matter. In a couple of conversations I heard of members who had allegedly engaged in malfeasance—for instance, in money matters. Yet even these people were given the benefit of the doubt by their pastors and finally forgiven. In one case a special act of forgiveness was undertaken in a worship service, with the pastor encouraging and leading it.

Some told stories about times when they placed major responsibility in the laps of lay leaders and stepped back. Sometimes they did so because there was too much for the pastor to do. More often, though, the pastor knew that the person or team was better equipped than the pastor to do the task at hand.

What I call a "perception of equitable care" is important to this dimension of trust. If the pastor has favorites, chooses to spend more time with some than others, always relies on this or that leader without considering others, defends some while seeming to give up on others, trust will be tested. It is not that the pastor must plan a social life that includes everyone in the parish. But fairness in the church is of utmost importance. Fairness tells people they can trust the pastor. Balance is the key. It is important for congregational health that pastors work deliberately to show fairness. Some pastors spoke with authentic humility about the trust members feel:

- "They love me, but I don't know how they tolerate me."
- "I don't have to tell people 'I am your leader.'"
- "I have always felt there was someone out there in the congregation who could do anything I do better than I can."

- "They discovered that my love for God and the church is real because I have been willing to risk."

A give-and-take prevails between pastor and parishioners about the
pastor's prophetic role. While these pastor-leaders were willing to step
out prophetically when necessary, they did not say that their pastoral
ministry depended on it. Some experienced analysts of pastoral ministry
contend that for a pastor to last long years in a congregation with integrity
intact, he or she must have won a "gunfight" at some point. That is,
pastors must have shown a kind of courage that stands above the norm,
calls others to risk, yet doesn't take itself too seriously. Whether or not
a major win is important, it is vital that the pastor be known as one with
conviction who will not compromise what matters.

The trusted pastor has been willing to take risks while conveying
the conviction that he or she did nothing that others would not also be
willing to do. Above all, the pastor will say that such risk-taking is not
a characteristic of the person but a result of God's call and power.

One pastor said, without any apparent trace of self-praise, "I have
not violated their trust." This fact is most evident when there has been
tension, conflict, and division, and the pastor was there both to guide the
conversation and to give voice to important principles. To violate trust
would be to lie, to say one thing and mean another, to tell one person
yes and another no. Congruency of word and deed, of stated intention
and later action, are vital to building and holding trust. People can forgive differences, I was told, if matters are handled with integrity. All in
all, to trust and be trusted is critical to effective pastoral ministry.

A crucial role change from the past is that effective management of
interpersonal trust has, until recently, seemed enough. Now, however,
the pastor must be sensitive to corporate trust, willing to take steps to
build mutual confidence between the people as a body and the pastor.

Committed to a Future of Hope

> Then afterward
> I will pour out my spirit on all flesh;
> your sons and your daughters shall prophesy,
> your old men shall dream dreams,
> and your young men shall see visions.
>
> (Joel 2:28)

This commitment to the future concerns vision and the visionary. Some pastors were clear about not being "visionary" themselves. This is why I emphasize a broader "commitment to the future" rather than "being visionary." Such a commitment may involve being a visionary person, or it may mean that the pastor makes it part of her craft to seek out and open the doors for lay visionaries in the congregation. In either case, there is a commitment to tomorrow, an unwillingness to stop thinking about it.

"It is important to be forth-telling," said one pastor. Forth-telling calls people to the future. "People look for visionary leadership..."

Among the stark differences in the emerging church is people's expectation that leaders call them to struggle with tomorrow. I am convinced that clergy often underestimate the laity in this regard. We believe they are basically satisfied with just doing things as they have done them, maintaining the status quo. The old mantra "We've always done it this way" may be said more by pastors than by laity.

The coming reality is that younger persons are asking the church to create a vision of tomorrow. "The person in leadership needs to be clear about expectations regarding the future." But people won't accept this vision from just anyone. They are willing, however, to hear from pastors who care for them. "Because I will listen, they trust me to call them back."

It is important, I heard, for the church to be in a partnership of vision with the pastor-leader. Said one: "Vision-casting and vision-catching are mutual." There is no point in a pastor's giving voice to a vision of the church's future direction if there's no one to hear and become excited by it.

So being visionary, whether one is the actual vision-caster or enables others to assume this role, is not enough. A congregation needs to be called to the vision, indeed, to the future. Furthermore, a vision stated in terms too lofty to be grasped by the congregation is useless.

I had been preaching with some frequency about the importance of caring for the poor, particularly for those whose skin color differs from ours. The Smith family—nice, hard-working people in and out of the church—let me know they were leaving the church. "Why?" I asked, shattered, taking their departure personally. I discovered that I *should* take it personally. They said, "We are tired of being called bad and racist and mean." Rather than beginning where they were, I had been wanting them to leap ahead to the place where I thought they should be. They said, "No thank you."

One pastor commented, "I have to give voice to stimulate the dialogue." The dialogue is vital to a congregational vision. Visions articulated but not owned by the members are wasted. Being a visionary pastor should not be confused with being a lonely prophetic figure isolated from reality.

The truth is that many laypeople yearn for visionary leadership. Perhaps this is why some, at least, have followed articulate leaders into crazy actions like the mass "Heaven's Gate" death pact of those who believed they were going to follow the Hale-Bopp comet. This strange and tragic event shows the extreme form of an urge that lives in many of us, to see and grapple with the future in a way that calls us to commitment at any cost.

"You see it from the Lord, and the people then do it," said one pastor. While this statement may at first reading seem incredibly naive, it does capture a seeking side of people. Faith-based folk seem at once to be both enormously self-sufficient and in need of direction, both autonomous and wanting authority in life. The hunger for meaning becomes more believable as we read of people following bizarre and destructive courses to show their commitments. If the church is to have credibility in these meaning-starved times, it must have a word to say to this contemporary quest for direction.

I heard the pastor-leaders speak of Bible studies, prayer groups, training in spiritual disciplines, vital fellowship, challenging program opportunities, and other entry points for people seeking a view of the future. "Visions, themselves, tend to be surprisingly simple . . . they begin as . . . a 'strategic umbrella' under which specific steps can be worked out," Jay Conger avows.[13] We are not talking about something terribly complex, but about a willingness to risk sharing dreams, giving voice to hopes and wants to which God leads us.

This way of being the church must be seen in contrast to a church that places its highest value in making people feel at home, comfortable, safe, secure. Many congregations, through the brief but hardy "salad days" of the 50s, and the decades of stress and change since then, have chosen to be bastions of sameness, rather than places where the people of God are challenged to look to tomorrow. In the process many gifted pastors have become keepers of the status quo rather than heralds of

God's emerging realm. Often this is what has been expected of them. The new role of the pastor-leader was well described by one who said, "To some I tell too much truth."

This role of visionary is a new one for the average pastor. Using the image of shepherd, we have thought of ourselves only as keepers of the flock, not as those with eyes pointed toward the horizon, looking for dangers and fresh fields. Today, visionary and future-oriented leaders are called for.

The Mission-Focused Pastor

Mission is the way a congregation and pastor understand and describe the future to which they are committed. It draws them, almost like a magnet, to itself. Some call this style "mission-driven." My conversations with these men and women lead me to call it "mission-compelled." The difference is between being pushed and being pulled. This mission given to the congregation by God has them in thrall, and there is no choice but to head in its direction.

Living in the present, the congregation is continually beckoned to the future that this mission helps them glimpse. In his study of theology of mission, David Bosch says, "Living in the creative tension of, at the same time, being called out of the world and sent into the world, [the church-in-mission] is challenged to be God's experimental garden on earth, a fragment of the reign of God...a pledge of what is to come."[14] The church lives now, but it reaches toward the hope of that fulfilled mission of tomorrow.

One pastor put it simply: "The best of us must help the rest of us till the rest of us are the best of us." These words set forth a potent statement of where we are drawn, yet an equally clear one of what we must do *now* to get there.

"Our church is a church with an attitude—joy, openness, justice," claimed another. In these three words, we hear the bringing together of who we are now with a sense of where we are to go.

"When we surrender ownership of the church to God, we have responsibility for the fruit," one pastor acknowledged. Many pastors spoke similarly, not passively eyeing the future while waiting for God to bring it about. None would be guided by the old camp poem, "God has no hands but our hands, to do God's work today," for all know that God has infinite ways of working and doing. All of them would agree that we are called not to be at rest, but to do our best.

One pastor stated it powerfully: "The pastor's job is not taking care of people, but leading them into mission." The greatest qualitative difference between these pastors and prominent pastors I met when I was entering ministry is that these men and women see their role to minister as much to the church and its mission as to individual members. Pastoral care is certainly important to them. Their average tenures are testimony to this commitment, because pastors do not stay in churches for long years unless they give strong pastoral care to people. But whereas for many in earlier eras this pastoral care was the greatest strength *and* the one people wanted most, the preference is changing. Today in a growing way people want that second strength, a capacity to lead the whole people in their shared mission as God's people in this place, just as much as they want the first, personal pastoral strength. Corporate trust is becoming as important as personal trust.

Several pastors spoke sincerely of the need for the congregation to be engaged in a continuing process of discernment of the congregation's mission. One said, "They will listen carefully to me. They will also test this against their own listening. And they will discern the call for the body." It is as though the congregation needs a conversion or transformation experience just as individual believers do. The congregation's mission is taken seriously by these pastors. Not all of the congregations are in the same place in this regard. Some, closer to corporate transformation, may tend to listen more for the pastor's voice to lead. But a number of the pastors, sensitive to the perils of such dependency, seek to help the people use spiritual disciplines not only to discern their personal faith journeys but the congregation's journey as well.

Congregations differ in the nature of their missions. The historically African-American congregations have tended to be more overtly engaged in their communities in confronting the structures that chew people up, so to speak. Two great and historic congregations in Baltimore have proud histories of involvement in important movements to acquire rights for disenfranchised former slaves and their descendants. In Washington, D.C., some congregations are active in addressing the complex and, some would say, devious, political world that occupies the city.

Several historically "Anglo" congregations are focused on being inclusive centers of hospitality, places where all people are welcomed. A few of these churches have become multi-ethnic as a result of this openness and have had to confront their communities courageously with the results of the all-too-frequent exclusiveness that still plagues society.

A number of congregations have chosen to focus on one outreach theme for the long haul. One California congregation has become a center for housing renewal; it is involved each year in several construction programs. When church members built a major addition to their facility, they had it designed for easy conversion from educational space to a homeless shelter and back, depending on the season and need.

Several congregations place less emphasis on corporate action in outward mission and more on encouraging members to engage the world where they live, work, study, and play. "Our mission is to equip and mobilize people to be involved where they are," said one pastor.

To have a mission does not mean that a congregation's focus must be on outreach. Outreach is only one way mission can be lived out. One congregation, which has established an after-school facility where children can study in safety, centers its mission on being a teaching church. There people receive not only basic biblical study skills; they can also do seminary-level studies of text and theology. Another congregation sees and lives its mission as becoming a highly visible witness for Christ in the larger community. To do this, members use all means available, from public media to street theater, to call attention to Christ's love.

Many pastors have learned that a mission is only as vital as the strategies developed to carry it out. A number of congregations have learned strategic planning to help them move from words to work, from dreams to deeds.

It is hopeful and dramatic to hear and see the degree to which these congregations have become committed to their place in God's ongoing creation. They bear out the reality that the church of today will live into tomorrow only if it is eager and willing to take risks to reach from its own "doorsteps to the ends of the earth," in the words of one denomination's mission imperatives.

Committed to Shared Leadership

Every pastor with whom I spoke was willing to take major risks as a
leader. I was struck by their clear commitment at this point. One said,
for example, "My growing edge is to take greater risks in modeling and
helping us 'correct' one another." This willingness to step out doesn't
seem to come from ego need, but from a depth of spirituality and courage.

At the same time, every pastor gives witness to the importance of
sharing leadership. They said: "We do not do things individually" and
"We work as a team. It's the only way to go."

Eighteen of the 32 described their preferred leadership style as
"collaborative." Several others identified this style and one other, with
"facilitative" and "selling" mentioned an equal number of times, as
being of equal importance to them.

When asked about the leadership styles of "telling" and "selling"
(or persuasion, witnessing, convincing), several gave these two a positive interpretation, and said they use these styles when appropriate.
"Truth-telling," as distinguished from "telling," will be discussed in the
next part of this chapter, but the pastors did not take well to describing
"telling" and "selling" with such images as bossiness, autocratic action,
power-pushing, and manipulation. They value persuasion, witnessing,
and sharing convictions. If these actions fall into the categories of telling
and selling, then so be it. The pastors are willing to be "tellers" and
"sellers."

Entrepreneurship is valued, particularly in newer congregations.
Indeed, pastors of the newer churches all said that churches don't get
started without it. The pastor has to have this spirit in the ways he or she
works, and be willing to speak out in a bold and brassy manner in an-
nouncing the presence and declaring the purpose of this new community.

But the greatest consensus about leadership is that the shared style
is at the core of day-in-day-out leading in the church's life. The pastors
said this clearly:

- "There is never a major decision without the ministers and elders
  being on board."
- "I get scared when I work alone."
- "Mutual trust is vital."
- "Without partnership we can do nothing."

Well practiced, this shared leadership can be almost an art form. "We have learned to build on each other's ideas. We try hard not to be attached to our own thinking." How can such disinvestment in one's "own thinking" happen in this age when so many spend time and effort looking out for "number one"? Again, it is a spiritual matter. If God's work is at stake here, then what each person thinks, no matter how attractive it may have seemed when the thought first came, must often yield to the community's sense of where God is leading.

Many pastors have a clear sense that God speaks in the voice of the church. If the people look faithfully at their call, then God will be known through that shared voice.

It must be emphasized again, though, that not one of these pastor-leaders shuns the responsibility of leading alone if a time or situation should call for it. All people of strong faith trust God's presence and power. But the pastors' clear preference is for leadership to be shared and they may, at most, sometimes be first among equals. One pastor said she spends "a lot of time just getting out of the way so others can lead."

The pastor-leader will be aware of various leadership styles, and will learn to use them when needed and appropriate, but will generally work hardest to build a collaborative approach to leadership.

Committed to Truth-Telling

Here is one place where the pastor's leadership role is unique.

One pastor declared, "To me, to share a vision is not 'selling,' like a hard-nosed hustler. It is sharing the very depths of my soul, laying myself bare before them. I'll be damned if someone can tell me that is 'selling.' That has come out of the struggle of my life. This is *passion*. There is a sacred call here."

In varying degrees of intensity, all pastor-leaders said that telling the truth is essential to their way of leading. Whether in pulpit, prayer circle, planning meeting, or personal conference, times will come when the pastor-leader has to declare the unwelcome truth. As one put it, "Courage to speak the unpopular or tough word is appreciated."

Many of these pastors speak of having found that others in the church do respond to truth-telling, whether it is in the "taught word," the "teaching of new people," the "teaching of old people," preaching, or any other setting in the church. Look at an example.

Two neighboring pastors of the same denomination undertook, with no collaboration, to tell what they each held to be the truth about Christian values and the crisis of racism in their community and the land. Recent events and community uprisings had made this the main issue of the day, as these two saw it. Not only in their preaching, but in pastoral conversations, youth group discussions, property use decisions, and any other available places, they told what they were convinced was truth *and* they invited others to do the same. Both congregations struggled with this truth-telling, and both pastorates were terminated as a result of it, but many lives and opinions were affected. Neither pastor looked back with regret about their actions.

Looking again at Mark 1:22, which says that Jesus "taught as one having authority," we must wonder: What gives pastor-leaders authority? The stories I heard were of pastors whose credibility is high. They are trusted. They are heard. They are not always agreed with but they are respected.

These pastors are truth-tellers and foster a climate of mutual truth-telling. This doesn't mean that everyone sits around somberly confessing. Hardly. The faith communities I heard about are places where people respect others and don't demand a brutal disgorging. But the pastor's example of honesty, a willingness to confront and genuinely struggle with truth and its fallout, whether the truth of a Scripture text or an interpersonal process, is a behavior extremely important to that pastor's credibility.

If a pastor says one thing and does another, makes promises with no apparent intention of keeping them, avoids grappling with his or her own deepest dilemmas, refuses to hear and accept feedback, preaches and teaches pablum instead of solid food, always takes the focus away from the other person and brings it to the self, then truth-telling is not present. So "truth-telling," as these pastors spoke of it, is not something that stands in simple contrast to "lie-telling." It is, rather, the pastor's desire to preach what will be practiced, and when the people understand this, then this leader's stripes will have been earned.

I cannot overemphasize the importance of this quality. It has been said in the past that one pays dues (I prefer to use the words "wins trust") in a pastorate by shepherding the people faithfully. Manipulation is a possibility, for in some instances pastors could call on the shut-ins, tend the sick, and be present at times of passage just to win the support of parishioners. If that is the way dues were paid yesterday, then in a growing number of churches today trust is gained by both personal pastoral sensitivity and truth-telling. Done together, they cannot be manipulative. The new pastor for a new time needs to struggle and grow in both ways.

Attuned to the World

The pastor-leaders said in almost every conversation that they and the church need to be aware of the world around them. With all its bumps and bruises, warts and wants, its possibility and promise, this is a world that God is creating and still loves passionately. An old friend and partner in ministry, Charles Bayer, said 30 years ago when renewal of the church was coming into vogue that "God is not, finally, out to renew the church. God wants to renew the world."

As an example of being in touch with the world, many pastors and their congregations have embraced the arts. One congregation has become a thriving center for the arts in its city, with artists and artisans finding a home in the church, having often come from viewing the church as suspect, if not downright hostile to the arts.

A number of pastors and congregations value technology and see it offering valuable tools to be learned and used. Though I didn't count the number of Web pages among the 32 churches, likely there are many. Churches have fruitfully made use of expertise in the pews to help use technology for faith's purposes and practices.

The pastors know that the church must be aware of the terrible pain in so much of the world. Several of these congregations live out inclusiveness as well as making it a goal. They know that people of certain ethnic or economic groups or sexual preferences have not been welcomed in the church before.

In the near future, churches in America will be challenged in major ways to take responsibility for the poor. Because of recent policy changes by governments, those whose calling is to care for the poor, the neglected, and the ignored will need to assume new levels of commitment to reach them with help.

The pastor-leaders we hear from are, in many cases, positioned with their congregations to move rapidly to richer ministries of caring. One said: "The spirituality of being 'other-centered' is growing." Another said: "Early on, there was not a lot of interest in associating with people not like them. Now getting involved is getting around."

One pastor spoke of the pastor's emerging role this way: "Shepherds do not win sheep. Sheep win sheep." This concept applies to outreach as well as evangelism. The pastor's task is to focus on equipping the laity to give witness to their faith, especially to those excluded from full acceptance.

This attitude differs from earlier times because the church doesn't have time to wait for the larger community to accept the oppressed. In the past, progress toward a level playing field generally began in the public arena. Now the church must assume leadership, because the world outside the church has not maintained progress in breaking down the walls that separate people.

In Conclusion

Significant role changes for pastors are obvious in this discussion of leadership for the future church. The pastor, who once was assessed on spiritual matters primarily by how he or she led public worship, will be expected to become deeply embedded in spiritual disciplines of prayer, meditation, dialogue, Bible study, and silence.

The pastor, whose trust was once evaluated mainly on one basis— how he or she cared pastorally for individuals in crises—will find trust being assessed in more complex ways. Trust will grow if he or she is willing to trust. A capacity to develop corporate as well as individual trust, will become more important.

The pastor, once called as a generalist who did preaching, teaching, pastoral, and administrative functions well, will be called to care in a visionary way as much about tomorrow as today.

The pastor, who once was secure in the position if he or she could just keep things running smoothly, will be asked to help people become compelled by their mission, the call God places on them for tomorrow.

The pastor, who could often go it alone (and wanted to), will be called to be a partner, offering resources and skills as part of a team.

The pastor, who could use well-chosen words to cover just about any situation, will be asked to bring honesty and expertise, not just opinions. The pastor will need to be a truth-teller.

The pastor, who could do well simply by being attuned to needs in the congregation, must be ready to hear the world beyond the congregation, its weaknesses and strengths, problems and possibilities.

The pastor, who was once one of the town's most respected people, must now learn to live with doubters, skeptics, opinionated persons, and those who don't have a clue but who need community anyway.

Roles and demands are changing. Unless pastors are prepared for a new time, the church as we know it will pay a high price. Let's be ready for this new day, for according to the testimony of 32 pastors, it is not only coming, it is here. I cannot state too strongly the truth that there is yet time for change in this direction. But this time is not endless.

CHAPTER 6

Renewing the Pastor's Vocation

Therefore, since it is by God's mercy that we are engaged in this ministry, we do not lose heart. . . . But we have this treasure in clay jars, so that it may be made clear that this extraordinary power belongs to God and does not come from us.

(II Cor. 4:1, 7)

What will the pastor's vocational world be like in coming decades? This book has examined pastors whose current ministries point in important directions. These pastors are trying to discern the present and coming concerns of the church and world, and to respond with leadership that will help the church be faithful to God. It is my hope that much can be learned from these findings.

Before closing the book, though, I believe it essential that we try to understand the pastor. What compels her to go into ministry? What makes him give himself to work that can be stress-producing, energy-draining, and often thankless? How can this vocation be renewed?

An Act of Renewal

"I renew my confession of faith in Jesus Christ as Lord, and my ordination vows, and commit myself to being one of your pastors, to working in partnership with pastor colleagues here and in the whole church and with all of the lay ministers in this congregation," said Rachel Frey at her installation as associate minister of University Church.

It was a brief but powerful act of covenant, a time to hear once

more God's calling of a person to the vocation of ordained ministry.
This young minister, only four years out of seminary, had been invited to
become part of the pastoral team leading a congregation of nearly 300
active members. She was both eager for this call and concerned that she
not disappoint God and those who had called her. She also knew that
late 1997, when she was called and installed, was very different from
1990, when she first experienced an urge to prepare for ministry. The
world had changed, and she had grown and changed.

Rachel will work in partnership with Marshall, a seasoned pastor,
who has served this congregation for nearly 24 years. The church is
made up of people in higher education at a state university nearby,
federal government personnel, and others mostly in service vocations.
Most are well-educated, progressive, and ready to reach out to the larger
community and world. Christian education is important here.

The congregation's time together is meaningful, whether people
gather for a fellowship period after worship, a big dinner, or a home-
grown dramatic performance. Members' talents and contributions are
lifted up as important. University Church is a lively place, appealing to
people of all ages, yet facing a future that will test the congregation's
commitment to the values of community, education, outreach, and pastoral care. That testing begins with a community in transition, an aging
building, and a changing base of members. Those who formed the congregation nearly 40 years ago are growing old or gone. Their children
and many newer people form the congregation's membership and leadership core now. The needs of these youth and young adults are far more
complex than in past times.

What will life and ministry be like for Rachel, now in her late
twenties? It might help Rachel if we could find all the answers and hand
them to her wrapped and guaranteed. What we *can* do is ask some of the
right questions and pose possible visions that will help us discern the
direction Rachel and others will need to go if theirs is to be faithful and
effective ministry.

One reality of Rachel's life in ministry is that she will be watched.
While people may be less interested than before in her personal life,
there may be more who observe to see how she studies, prays, preaches,
coaches, shares visions, and leads. Her use of power will be scrutinized.
"They don't trust a minister who wants to overpower the congregation,"
said one pastor.

Rachel, like many who will serve in pastoral ministry well into the 21st century, will be expected to fulfill roles that ministers in the past have not had to consider. Life is changing, if only because we live in a time of growing technological advancement and massive competition from such nonreligious appeals as movies, round-the-clock TV sports, and singles bars. How can we articulate the new roles of pastors in this era?

Looking Out from the Inside

An overused image is that ordained ministers live in a fishbowl. Our vocation is public. When one lives in a glass fishbowl, much of what happens is seen by those who look in from outside.

But what if we change the worn image and imagine looking *out* from *inside* the fishbowl? How does the world around the pastor look to the pastor? What's out there? We will not agree on all that we see. But several sights were confirmed by conversations with the 32 pastors I interviewed, and by reflections from dozens of others with whom I have worked.

To understand these characteristics of the world is to know why many people have entered the ministry. Few of the pastors with whom I spoke referred to mystical reasons for their choice of vocation. But a good number did talk of wanting to make a difference in the lives of people and in the world. They told of believing that God had given them talents and gifts that could be of particular use, and that somehow they knew God was calling them to this vocation. Trying to look at life around them through their eyes will give us added insight into why they are in ministry and into role changes required of these pastors as they continue to try to offer God's healing through their vocation.

Yearning for Salvation

The idea of yearning for salvation is deeply rooted in biblical theology. This yearning is akin to hunger for spiritual direction, but it precedes that. The pastors talked about it this way:

- "We talk about our sins and hopes, all in the open.
- "People seek something special, to connect with something beyond themselves."
- "We aren't just doing something to be church; we are connected to the source of life."
- "Our commitments to Jesus as Lord and Saviour made our mutual commitment possible."   ·
- "Our focus is to bring people into relationship with Jesus Christ and each other."

The root of the word *salvation* in Hebrew Scriptures sounds something like "shua." It means "space." A core meaning of salvation for the Hebrew people was that God gives people space, room to live and grow. Among the eloquent passages of praise to God is this one from Psalm 66:12b, "You have brought us out to a spacious place." To be liberated from narrow to open space was an important part of what the Hebrews meant by salvation. Israel may seem a narrow land to us, but to people who had been cruelly enslaved in the far narrower Nile River Valley, it was "a spacious place." It was salvation.

This was the salvation theology Jesus learned as he grew to maturity. This is what the church proclaims, as people find by God's grace the space to forgive and be forgiven of sin, to live in redeeming community, to grow in understanding of themselves and others, and to be liberated from a captivity that makes them preoccupied only with themselves.

The pastors said that people want this liberation, this space. They may not always be able to name it, but they know when they experience it. "Why else," one asked, "would there be a church, but to make this kind of difference in people's lives? If not for this, then they might as well join a civic club and make business connections, or a fraternal organization and learn rituals, or a service organization and do good deeds."

The pastor's role is to be the master-teacher of salvation theology. For years, pastors of many mainstream churches hesitated to use religious words outside of worship and other designated "safe" situations. One pastor asked his congregants to speak unashamedly of the Gospel to friends, family, and strangers, but he could never do so himself. What these pastors told me was that it is time to move beyond hesitation to proclaim the truth that God sets us free. They are in this vocation not to

keep quiet about their faith, but to name it and claim it publicly. For
them the pulpit, the study group, and the personal conference are all
places where people are invited to struggle with that which gives meaning to life, their salvation.

Hunger for Spiritual Direction

It follows, they said, that people who search for meaning also seek a way
by which they can "stay on course," as one pastor phrased it. In nearly
all of the congregations pastors pointed to a need for visible leadership
that "uses the words of the spirit." A pastor of a nondenominational
church spoke of his congregation as a place where unchurched people
find an entry point back into the faith. "Many were alienated from the
church as children or youth. It may have been years since they've been
in a congregation. But they find themselves yearning for spiritual nurture. We try not to give an impression of organizational superstructure or
bureaucracy. Many, after a time of being in a faith community again
here, move to more structured denominations, sometimes to the church
that they left, now feeling far less threatened by them." Underlying
their entry into the church, though, is that hunger for direction in a community that will meet and move with them at an appropriate pace. For
many, I heard the pastors say, spiritual direction involves *both* guidance
and supportive presence on the journey.

A special quality of many of these pastors is a patient willingness to
meet people where they are. Several pastors said that in their own faith
journeys they learned how *not* to be as spiritual directors. They were at
times pushed to become almost immediately what others wanted them
to be. For their own pastoral ministries they chose a way of teaching,
coaching, urging, modeling, and accompanying that can help others
without repelling them.

This way of bringing guidance and presence together is particularly
important, given the urgency in people's lives. Though pain is not new
in human experience, the stresses brought on by the information revolution and a resulting depersonalization, an increased incidence of such
diseases as AIDS, substance abuse dependency, the growing pressure of
poverty in the midst of plenty, and other contemporary facts of life appear to be making many people feel more urgently the need for God's
presence.

The pastors are determined that the church be a place where all people can find a hospitable spiritual home. At the same time it is important in most of the churches that all who enter are also encouraged to undertake a disciplined lifelong journey of growth in the Spirit through study, prayer, worship, interpersonal dialogue, and other means.

If the church is to be a special place, the pastor must provide an example by guiding and accompanying people on their journeys. One pastor commented, "People trust me to lead because of my willingness to hear [and] intuit, and they have come to trust me for a 'living word that is timely.' " This pastor speaks for many.

The church is more than a place. A place cannot respond to the spiritual hunger of which the pastors spoke. The church must be led by a person who practices responsiveness to spiritual hunger, first by actively seeking nurture for his or her own hunger, and then by reaching to nourish the hunger in others.

Once again we see the centrality of spiritual discipline for the pastor. Though many have long practiced prayer and Bible study, in recent years more have broadened their spiritual lives to include spiritual guidance, silent retreats, meditation, theological reflection, and other disciplines. Further, members increasingly ask for guidance in these disciplines. Where public worship and invocations and benedictions at committee meetings have often been the only attention given to spiritual matters, churches are seeing an increase in both the practice of the disciplines and the training of laypeople in their use.

Wounded Lives

The woundedness of which so many pastors spoke characterizes people of all ages, beginning with the young. It covers a range of pain far wider than only that of physical illness.

Perhaps the youth group that one pastor described can illustrate this woundedness. He works alongside the lay adult sponsors, believing it important for youth to know and have access to him as pastor. Four out of five of the young people are in single-parent or second-marriage homes. Several were born to unmarried parents. A good number have been involved in counseling for substance abuse, and nearly all have been pressured to try drugs. One-third smoke or have smoked cigarettes;

breaking the habit is a subject of great debate among them. Most have been to parties in homes where alcohol flowed freely with no adults present. Some have friends who struggle with alcoholism. Two have been incarcerated and are on parole, one for acts involving violence. The pastor spoke of one young man's suburban senior high class, where 125 students volunteered to give blood for the first time. Sixteen percent of the students were found to be HIV-positive. "Behind the joviality, casual rap, Ping-Pong, and prep talk," he said, "are some young men and women carrying heavy loads." Comparable examples could be cited in all age groups.

Another pastor said, "You folks from judicatories are always out to give us training in stewardship, program planning, how to teach Sunday school, and so forth. What we need is training in how to talk with people whose homes are falling apart, whose kids have gotten into drugs and casual sex, whose brothers and sisters have AIDS, and whose jobs are caving in."

The pastors spoke of their own search for ways to respond to hurting lives. Many entered pastoral ministry to do more conventional kinds of pastoral care. Yet today the least of their needs is for tools to help those who are more conventionally ill. For while heart attacks, cancer, pneumonia, and other illnesses can be harsh and fatal, leaving grief in their wake, most pastors are trained to minister in such situations. Now they are called to equip themselves to reach out as pastors to people with less predictable needs.

Several pastors have sought assistance from pastoral counseling centers, community centers, specialized health services, and other resources. Some are drawing upon the health care field to add to their staffs, with parish nurses the most frequent innovation.

An emerging pastoral role is as broker of such resources. For while pastors have long been encouraged to refer people to counselors and psychiatrists, not too many have done so. In seeing this "broker" role emerge, we find pastors redefining the traditional assumption that a pastor can and should be all things to all people. This new role promises more effective ministry and more realistic use of the pastor's time and skills.

A Broken World

If individuals' pain were not enough, the pastors see a world where things fall apart. In these pastors' lifetimes the world has become a place where there are few surprises. Particular issues trouble each of them. Some, of all races, see growing racism as a scourge to be faced. Others have deep convictions about the widening gap between affluence and need. Some identify political, class, and religious intolerance and polarization, as well as incivility and resultant conflicts as nasty signs of the times. Nearly all decry the abuse of the created order as an expression of human arrogance.

The pastors see these abuses not just as social processes, but as violations of God's creation. They do not take on these great crises as causes, even though all would agree that humanity is making a mess of things. It is important to see that these pastors respond to the need to do something about these destructive forces as part of God's larger work. Said one, "The world is broke. But only God can fix it. We have responsibility. But we have spent too much time thinking *we* could fix *God's* creation."

Lest we conclude that this view represents a denial of responsibility, we need to know that most of the pastors work hard at the healing of the community and world. One served as a member of the city's school board. Another is active in county politics, not to promote certain candidates but as an arena in which to focus her commitment to justice. Another works very hard at international bridge-building through religious, government, and nongovernmental organizations. Another led her congregation to protest a U.S. government institution that trains military leaders of Latin American nations. Another led his congregation to challenge other city churches to join in addressing gangs and their growing power. Another asked his congregation to sponsor and house a day care center for the infant children of young women trying to complete high school. Another uses biblical resources to train members to confront a city's decaying political system and the myriad ways it abuses its citizens. Another has been a key leader in his congregation's housing ministry. While many entered pastoral ministry partly because it seemed a peaceful vocation, several have learned conflict-resolution skills to be peacemakers in their communities as well as within the congregation.

For all these pastors, the public-issue ministries they care about are faithful responses to difficult problems. They see these ministries as acts of obedience to God. These actions do not come, therefore, out of an orientation to causes as much as from the faith focus of the pastors and growing numbers of the laity.

In the past pastors have often felt it best to stay out of controversy; the risks may have been too high. Pastors may have been personally disinclined for various reasons, including ideology, to step out in public ways. Their congregations may have told them not to do so, that such matters are none of the church's business.

Most of the emerging pastors, though perhaps fearful of consequences, have not allowed fear to deter their obedience to God. Nor are they engaged in these issues only because they are favorite causes (though they may be), but because they are doing what they believe is the right thing, God's will for them. They have challenged their congregations to do the same. If that challenge is made not in a scolding way but as a call to servant ministry, then they find themselves joined by gifted and committed laypeople.

Rusty, Dying Religious Institutions

As a rule, these pastors are not among those who would say that the reign of God depends on the success of the institutions we serve. Institutional success, several told me, can be seen from two perspectives:

*   From the point of view of business prosperity, which means that increasing numbers of people, income, and other assets are goals of the church.
*   From a spiritual perspective, which requires that we ask, in one pastor's words, "Are lives being changed, people finding purpose, families and communities being helped and healed?"

Several pastors whose congregations were in the critical stage of the congregational life cycle when the pastorate began, and whose churches are now experiencing revitalization and a re-entry into the formation stage, have seen that institutional decay slowly kills. When a congregation becomes institutionally unstable, when its money, membership, programs, and property deteriorate, the congregation naturally becomes self-absorbed. People fear their church will die. The dilemma for members is that this self-focus is the very opposite of that which can renew a congregation's spiritual health.

The movement of a congregation from self-focus to health can be long and grueling. One pastor, after six years, is finally beginning to see her congregation make decisions and take steps free of the fear that long bound them to look out only for their own life. What a joy this is!

Another pastor related the satisfaction of celebrating 70 percent growth in the number of committed, involved members. For some, adding 35 people to the active rolls over seven years would seem negligible, but in this church, only 40-plus cared much at all before. "This is a great gift God has given us!" The pastor told me that one of their goals is to start a new congregation within the next decade. "It was when I realized that I had married more people than I had baptized, and buried more than I had welcomed, that I knew I needed help." He began to learn new skills which, combined with deep faith in God's power and presence, made a striking difference in his pastoral ministry and the life of that congregation.

The most notable role change here is from manager to manager-leader. Few congregations in the critical stage can afford more than one pastor on staff. That one pastor will find it essential to be both manager and leader. As discussed in the last chapter, these two roles differ in that the manager cares for what is happening now, while the leader looks to what should happen in the future. Some pastors need to learn both roles. Most are schooled, if at all, to be managers only.

Unfortunately, many seminaries have yet to learn that fewer and fewer of the congregations for which they train pastors are viable, stable institutions. Tomorrow's church will need pastors who are leaders more than managers.

I have mentioned the need to serve as pastor to the corporate life of the congregation as well as to individuals. Like any group of people, the gathered church has a personality which the pastor is called to know, celebrate, teach, and lead. If the pastor insists on being only a chaplain to the needs of individuals, the church can slowly die and no one will know until it is too late.

Need for Alternatives to Mediocrity

Several pastors spoke with deep feeling about people who need to have their sights lifted beyond ordinary things. This is especially true in big cities, where many suffer loneliness. For many, poverty produces desperation with no way out. Boredom and depression drives others down. These people need more—not thrills, excitement, or entertainment, but a message of hope.

A pastor said, "When I came here, [the members] weren't very sure of themselves. We do a good job of letting people know how important they and the church are to each other."

This message has particular meaning in African-American congregations. "We don't entertain people; we feed them in spirit," said an African-American pastor of a large urban congregation. "It is not easy for them to live, work, and go to school in a majority white city."

"We are committed to uplifting the oppressed. Some join because through our food and clothing ministries they felt cared for in a world that doesn't really care very much."

Other congregations encounter this need for uplifting also.

- "I like to be with people, to love people others have rejected, just being that simple element who says, 'Let's try it, let's risk, trust God.'
- "Most people work in jobs where they're told no. Most of the time things can be better than we ever thought they would be."
- "People don't just want more business. They seek something special."

The new role for pastors here is in calling the church to see the importance of offering a community that reaches beyond the common, that lives out the sacramental character of faith, in which the holy transforms ordinary things and makes them special. At first hearing this may sound like one more load of theological jargon. In real life it means helping see the difference made when God's grace, community, compassion, and hope come alive. This transformation can happen in such ways as helping the poor organize for self-help, offering youth support and permission to say no to drugs and promiscuity, helping laypeople learn how to become change agents in the church and community and training older people to make pastoral visits with the lonely and confined. These and many more servant ministries need to be understood as ways in which God's grace changes the ordinary to the extraordinary.

The Pastor's Vocation

These pastors stated that one reason they entered pastoral ministry was to respond to these issues. Of course, not every pastor named all six as of equal concern. But all said or implied that they were not called and ordained as ministers for indefinable reasons. One characteristic of highly motivated and effective pastors is that they believe themselves drawn by God into this vocation to make a difference in the world.

Another sign of effectiveness is the capacity to retool, to adapt and learn new skills necessary for changing times and roles. Jesus' statement is true for pastors and the need to understand new roles for new times: "Neither is new wine put into old wineskins; otherwise the skins burst, and the wine is spilled, and the skins are destroyed; but new wine is put into fresh wineskins, and so both are preserved" (Matt. 9:17). By God's grace and hard work some pastors who knew the old roles have been able to learn new ones as well, and thus be tomorrow's shepherds.

Understanding changing roles to respond more faithfully to the needs of God's world is central to ministry. The vital church cannot be led by pastors whose worldview and role perceptions remain as they were in even the recent past.

Steps for Pastors

For many years I naively labored under the assumption that all of us in ordained ministry wanted to change, grow, and develop new skills. I still believe that such a desire should not be unusual for clergy. It seems most natural that we as pastors would want for ourselves what we urge of lay members, not to "neglect the gift that is in you" (I Tim. 4:14).

But as one veteran pastor asked, "What if the shepherd doesn't want to change?" He serves as interim minister in a congregation all too typical of those in the breakdown and critical stages. His comment is a potent reminder that change can't be forced on anyone, including pastors, but also that congregations will not move to vitality if the pastor is unaware of the skills needed for this challenge.

Pastors can take steps to help themselves find personal renewal and to become better pastors. Such measures will be of increasing importance as pressures on churches continue to grow.

Training and Growth in Spiritual Disciplines.

This is the single most important source of vitality in the pastoral life for those 32 with whom I spoke. Each engages in some form of spiritual discipline, practicing the chosen activity with regularity and commitment.

An increasing number of organizations offer training in spiritual disciplines. A pioneer interfaith training organization is Shalem Institute, established in the early 1970s, and still providing high-quality training in various forms of meditation. For those interested, Shalem also offers training for spiritual directors.

One outgrowth of the opening up that resulted fromVatican II has been the availability of Roman Catholic resources in spirituality to people from other religious bodies. Thomas Merton, a modern pioneer in spirituality and religious experience, was accessible to non-Catholics even before his untimely death. Since then, his influence has grown through books and tapes. Another rich gift of this opening has been the extent to which great Christian mystics from the past, like Hildegard of Bingen, Teresa of Avila, and St. John of the Cross, are now, as it were, in the public domain. Thus their examples teach spiritual growth to a widening audience. Spiritual growth has now become part of the curricula of many traditional academic seminaries and other graduate schools, and is offered in more and more continuing education programs.

As a pastor enters a world of disciplines new to many traditional mainline churches, it is important that he or she not become distanced from parishioners. For many church members, spiritual disciplines are a foreign subject. While many younger people are asking for exposure to these ancient yet new disciplines, others may be threatened by the practices.

Such experiences are sought, first of all, for the pastor's own spiritual growth and development. Spiritual disciplines include a variety of activities. We can pray using many forms, alone or in groups. Theological reflection through Bible study or study of other faith resources can be practiced as a personal or group discipline. Either can be fruitful.

Rich forms of meditation have developed from Christian and other religious histories. Spiritual renewal events like Cursillo and Walk to Emmaus from the Episcopal and United Methodist churches have helped many find vitality of faith. The key to spiritual discipline is being open to God's power to bring about growth and change.

Give and Receive Collegial Support

Few people understand the challenges, difficulties, joys, and opportunities of a pastor better than another pastor. Yet often pastors are hesitant to enter into deep covenant with each other—out of competitiveness, fear of being exposed as weak or vulnerable, or reluctance to make time for such interaction.

Pastors, like others, want to be in control. Since much of the church's life seems beyond our control, why not keep a firm grip on ourselves where we can?

When they can move beyond a need to control, pastors can find help in the support they offer each other. This support can take different forms: biblical study groups, theological reflection groups, interfaith dialogue experiences of short- or long-term duration, prayer cells or partnerships, case study groups to do problem solving, sharing skills, being together as families in regular social ways, and gathering with pastors of similarly situated congregations.

My experience as a pastor to pastors suggests that pastors are often reluctant to take the lead in forming such groups. Yet few who become involved in them have regrets. No one can establish an ongoing group for me. It must be my choice that sets such a group in motion.

The benefits of colleague support networks far exceed the risks and liabilities. This was one source of support not utilized by many of the pastors with whom I spoke. Yet from personal experience and the observation of countless colleagues, I am persuaded that one of the best sources of renewal, skill-development, personal support, and the deepening of faith is others who have chosen this amazing, often frustrating vocation of pastoral ministry.

Learn, Learn, and Learn Some More

An encouraging sign in the vocation of pastoral ministry is the increasing number of pastors eager to improve their ministry skills. I met a pastor for breakfast recently, and when I arrived he was reading a book by Marcus Borg (*Jesus: A New Vision*, Harper Collins, 1991), whose writing has sparked fresh interest and inquiry into the person of Jesus Christ. I asked John to tell me about the book and how he planned to use it. He said it was first for his own learning, but that he intended to use it as a resource for parish study groups. John has been out of seminary for 20 years. Unlike John, some pastors at that stage have chosen to vegetate.

According to an apocryphal story circulated through my denomination, one pastor had eight years of sermons, moved every eight years, wore those pages out after three eight-year pastorates, and then left the pastoral ministry.

These contrasting examples—John the learner-teacher and that unnameable (and, one hopes, mythological) pastor who spent 24 years doing the same things in three parishes—offer a pair of mirrors for every pastor. In which do I see myself?

Many denominations require minimal continuing education for maintaining credentials to practice ministry. Having worked with several judicatory ministry oversight bodies, I find that those minimal requirements are of little help in encouraging pastors to improve their practice of the craft of pastoral ministry. Attention should be given to strengthening these requirements.

Beyond requirements, we in pastoral ministry need to enter a covenant with each other that we will seek for ourselves the same discipline that we ask of lay members: to continue learning the faith and its applications. From monasteries to training centers, from seminaries to universities, opportunities abound.

Pastors need to be assertive in asking for the time, back-up assistance, and resources to help accomplish this task. I have files of letters sent to congregations asking them to pay their pastors' costs for an annual continuing education retreat, examples of ways congregations can work out compensation with new pastors to include funds and time for annual and sabbatical educational leaves. But such intervention from a judicatory pastor is usually not enough to persuade the congregation's leaders. The pastor must speak up.

One of the most refreshing, if frustrating, parts of the interviews with the 32 pastors was having to work around their educational leaves. One was just going on a sabbatical; two others were returning in a week. A half-dozen had to schedule our conversations around conferences for new skill development. It was inconvenient—but how energizing to meet a group of pastors who care for improving their faith and ministry. It is no coincidence that these pastors are leaders of transformed or transforming congregations!

As pastorates are formed, a part of the contract to be treated with the same care as monetary compensation is continuing education. Too often this element is given short shrift and left for later attention. But sabbatical educational opportunities are harder to negotiate after the contracting period. To postpone negotiation of continuing education may give some people the impression that professional continuing education is less important than basic compensation packages. It is essential that continuing education be given equal importance with other terms being negotiated. This attention will not be paid unless the clergy believe it is important.

Pastors need new information about the church to do pastoral ministry effectively in coming years. They need to learn about the stages of a congregation's life (as discussed in chapter four), understanding change (from a theological as well as a strategic perspective), and new modes of preaching, teaching, and spiritual development.

It is fair that those of us who are entrusted with the vocation of pastoral ministry be asked to hold ourselves accountable for professional development and growth. If we have lost motivation to improve, then we might well seek assistance to discern why. It was not easy for any of us to attain academic, performance, and ordination credentials to practice ministry. These gains are too valuable to be allowed to deteriorate through inattention.

Self-Care and Care for Important Others

Beyond continuing education, other aspects of self-care need attention. Indeed, while judicatories may require continuing education, no external authority can require other kinds of self-care. No one can force me to exercise, rest, take time off, pursue constructive avocations, and pay attention to my family and friends. And no one else can do these things for me.

A generalization drawn from comments made by pastors in the long-pastorate studies of the early 1980s is that many who go into ministry do so because they like being depended on by others. In other words, needing to be needed is typical of ministers.

This trait can be useful or harmful for ministry. If the pastor recognizes it as a gift of ministry to encourage and empower others, it can be used positively. But if the pastor tends to work in a way that makes others dependent on him or her, a gift can become an impediment. If the gift is not used to help others grow for their sakes, the pastor is using it to justify his or her own need to be needed.

It is this very quality of ministers that most helps or hinders self-care. We become living examples of a distortion of one of Jesus' most familiar sayings, "It is more blessed to give than to receive" (Acts 20:35). With pastors this text too often becomes, "It is much easier to give than to receive."

The result is that families, congregations, and the pastors themselves are shortchanged. The losses can include faith, time, health, happiness, and personal and professional effectiveness.

Though I did not ask specifically about self-care, at least 25 of the 32 pastors interviewed referred to their practices. These range from running or jogging to the consistent claiming of a weekly day or two off, from going to movies to having a circle of friends not usually part of the congregation, from doing projects with their families to reading and pursuing cultural interests. These pastors said also that it was often from self-care that some of their most important personal change and growth has come. That such pastors can attend to self-care puts the torch to our excuses that we are too busy for other pursuits.

It is the pastor's own choice to take positive steps to improve the quality of his or her life and pastoral ministry. What if the shepherd doesn't want to change? If he or she does not, the cost will be borne by congregation, family, and community, as well as by the self. The pastor's self-neglect, while not criminal, is an ethical issue. Clergy neglect of families is particularly troubling.

Self-care is a theological and spiritual matter. Nowhere does it say in Scripture that to "deny" oneself (Mark 8:34) means to deprive, despise, or mistreat oneself. Because all of life is a gift, including our physical and spiritual selves, and certainly our families and friends, our stewardship of these gifts is at issue here.

Calling Denominations and Judicatories

If we don't pay attention to the future, we won't be there. The larger church needs to take seriously the reality that congregations are not at the same stages where they were 50, 30, or even 10 years ago. A major ecclesiological fact of the American church is that most congregations have lived long enough to be in the "breakdown" and "critical" stages of their lives. The support and resources made available to them need to fit their situations.

This reality would be easily absorbed if all aging congregations were tiny, family-sized communities, rural heirs of the circuit riders. The judicatory's delusion is that congregations that are still viable, contributing, and supportive in many ways will continue in that pattern forever. They will not. Most of them are only a few years from the breakdown and critical stages.

Our times can be new times for the church if we undertake the revitalization of threatened churches and initiate many more new churches. We can help do the former by equipping pastors to be the leaders the churches need. We can do the latter without waiting for huge amounts of money to buy property, because it is Christian community, not structures, that makes a new church come alive.

Don't Ask Congregations Only for What They Can Give

Be ready to give to congregations. Whether the perception is accurate, many believe that when the denomination comes calling, "All they want is our money." There is enough truth in this notion to give pause. Congregations don't always have much money to give. Church and mission-development people who scratch their heads and wonder why the giving isn't on the increase should acknowledge that many congregations have less money to give because they are smaller, older (in membership and life), and in need of far more help than ever. On the other hand, *not* to ask a congregation to support the larger mission of the church is to treat it like a patient. Not asking can reinforce the danger already discussed, that a congregation will become self-absorbed. While in the short run it may make me feel good to be told to hang on to what I have, it finally doesn't help my health, and I become so wrapped up in my own plight that reaching out to others becomes unimportant.

Understand the Stages of the Life Cycle

Most denominational work with congregations has been based on the assumption that the congregations that matter are those in the "stabilization" stage in the life cycle. After all, they are the ones that produce money, volunteers, and program ideas—and they don't require much attention. When congregations have not been stable, the intervention has often been framed in a "wish you had been stable" judgment. So congregations not producing money, volunteers, participants, and other fuel that keeps the denominational machinery running may feel subtly (or even blatantly) judged.

The research interviews conducted here support the hypothesis that the growing edge in congregational development in our day is mostly with *new* and *aging* congregations. To be sure, there are still congregations in the stabilization period, but even these are becoming aware of the need to take steps to renew their life. Most American congregations today are beyond the stabilization period—not because they have done something wrong, but because they are of a certain age.

Learn How to Help Where Congregations Need Help

Help can come in the form of education about congregational life, consulting assistance to revitalize programs, and linkages with congregations that have experienced similar stresses.

A growing number of models for establishing new congregations and revitalizing aging ones are being developed. They include the house church model, as well as these others:

- Nesting—a new congregation meets to worship within the space of a sponsoring church.

- Satellites—a congregation establishes more than one site for worship.
- Mission group—a group of founders moves out from a parent church to start a new congregation.
- Pastor/developer—a new-church pastoral specialist is hired to develop the new project.

All these methods are being used to establish new congregations. Most of the models predate today's denominations, and they are being revived in a time when funds for new churches are limited.

The newer field is revitalization of older churches. Whether entering into prayer for the will of God in this process or placing a pastor/redeveloper in the congregation in the "critical" stage, some fresh, exciting, and profitable methods are being found. A congregation's redevelopment is no more guaranteed than is the development of a new congregation, though so far more new churches than old ones are finding life. These percentages may change as more is learned about redevelopment, and as more pastors enter this challenging field of pastoral ministry.

Train, Support, and Trust Tomorrow's Shepherds

Here is the most important proposal I can make. These faithful, innovative men and women in parish ministry need our care, support, and confidence. Many of them need the trust of judicatory and denominational leaders. They are not renegades and troublemakers. They are among the prophets of our day. They need more support than criticism.

They are not only the "once" pastors in this book's title. Among them are the vanguard of the "future" pastors. Alongside the 32 I interviewed are many more doing similar creative ministry, and countless others who can and will. My own experience has been that the middle judicatory is primarily concerned with preservation and not with innovation.

Some would ask me, "Then why bother to try to change the judicatory?" Because even though people in my kind of ministry are often late to become savvy to change and creativity in the congregation, such need not be the case. I am convinced that the church will become a far different place, a true center of God's vital renewal of the world, if there is an expression of the church that cares, first and last, about the health and faithful lives of congregations and their pastors. It needs to be a step apart from the congregation, yet close enough to know, love, and serve the congregation and its pastor. This is the judicatory.

Making this notion a reality means forming a new partnership with pastors. The pastors can be the teachers, trainers, prophets, and visionaries who, by God's grace, lead in shaping the church for a new age. Their role is far more crucial for this bold future than that of judicatory leaders. Judicatory pastors, whether called bishops, superintendents, regional/conference ministers, executive/association secretaries, executive presbyters, or whatever, are not on the front lines of this new struggle, but we can be powerful agents in support of those who are.

This new partnership with pastors continually undergirded with prayer must recognize a pair of historic realities that may seem somewhat in conflict:

• That congregations and their pastors cannot exist alone. They need a larger expression of church that helps equip and hold them accountable, unites them for mission, and affirms them.

• That one of the primary reasons for the existence of an expression of "church," apart from the gathered worshipping and serving congregation, is to help the congregation and its pastor be faithful and strong (suggesting self-sufficiency).

In a congregation's life no decision is more important than who will be its pastor. This decision is made in different ways in the rich variety of church traditions. What is called for here cuts across all those ways: the larger church needs to invest much of its confidence and life in the local pastor.

Such an investment calls for accountability. Pastors must be willing to be accountable to the larger church, where they receive not only the credentials to practice pastoral ministry, but also the support, nurture, and community needed to minister effectively. It is appropriate as well for every middle judicatory to be accountable to the congregation through an oversight committee that works with each congregation in formation or revitalization. These committees need to work with congregations and pastors to establish goals, evaluate progress, determine ways and degrees of support, and make available judicatory resources as needed. This undergirding is critical to the future of the church.

A Word to Seminaries

The important place of the seminary in this challenge for the future cannot be overstated. Is it fair to say that the seminary, particularly one tied to a denomination, is expected to produce ministers trained to lead the denomination's churches? If this is so, and it should be, then the purpose of this appeal is simple: your denomination's churches are changing rapidly, and to continue serving them, you need to change parts of your curriculum.

The classics of seminary education are essential. Historic and contemporary biblical methodologies, historical and current theology, history and polity, pastoral care, and educational method—all are important.

But is anyone telling the students that most of the congregations they are going to serve will not be healthy, viable, successful, growing places? Is anyone saying that most healthy parishes are only four to six years away from decline?

Is anyone helping students understand that the emerging church is multi-ethnic, worshiping in nontraditional ways, and grappling with human and community dilemmas not even dreamed of a few decades ago?

Is anyone helping these students learn the difference between being managers and leaders? Are these students still being trained for an outdated age of psychologized religion, in which how we feel about ourselves and others is the main norm of faith?

Is anyone enabling them to experience the wonder of the mystics, of spiritual experience, of saying to God, "Break me, melt me, mold me, fill me, use me"?

Is anyone telling them that the Gospel is about congregations as well as individuals, that it is about a willingness to die to old ways of doing things so as to be born to new life?

The seminary has lived on the front line of innovation for much of the church's history. This role has not always been easy. Most seminaries are financed by the contemporary church. Change is not always perceived to be in the church's best interest. But the days of the church as it is are numbered. Today can be an exciting time to be on the front line of shaping tomorrow's shepherds.

A Reflection

Quite soon a very gifted African-American pastor will begin a new ministry with a historic, center-city congregation. The congregation has always been predominantly European-American, though it is now 20 percent African-American, Hispanic, Asian, or "other."

The congregation's most stable period ended some years ago. Some members had begun to wonder if they would survive these new times. Their pastor is moving from one of the most highly visible and successful pastorates, not only in his own denomination but in American Protestantism as a whole. This is a spellbinding challenge for pastor, congregation, and denomination.

If this pastorate becomes a vital one, it will help light the way into the new century for much of its city, indeed for its whole denomination. If the congregation is to be vital, both congregation and pastor must hold fast to a deep confidence that God is with them as they walk this journey together.

Success may call for approaches different from those to which both pastor and congregation have become accustomed. Large numbers of new members may need to make room for hospitality to street people and undocumented aliens. A traditional youth ministry may have to move over to make room for a school rooted in Christian values.

The changes will be massive, or this new pastorate will disappoint many, beginning with God. Pray for this pastorate and all coming pastorates, that tomorrow's shepherds will know, accept, and live the new roles that are theirs.

We may be moving into the most dramatic and faith-filled time in the story of the Christian faith. How blessed we are to be alive now. How challenged we are to be faithful to the call.

NOTES

Chapter 1
1. Loren B. Mead, *The Once and Future Church* (Washington, D.C.: the Alban Institute, 1991), 43.
2. Nancy Tatom Ammerman, *Congregations and Community* (New Brunswick, N.J.: Rutgers University Press, 1997), 36.

Chapter 2
1. Alvin Toffler, *Future Shock* (New York: Random House, Inc., 1970), 11.
2. Wade Clark Roof and William McKinney, *American Mainline Religion* (New Brunswick, N.J., 1987), 22.
3. Dean Hoge, Patrick McNamara, and Charles Zech, *Plain Talk About Churches and Money* (Bethesda, Md.: the Alban Institute, 1997).
4. *Webster's Universal Dictionary and Thesaurus* (Montreal: Tormont Publications, 1993).
5. Hans Kung, *On Being a Christian* (Garden City, N.Y.: Doubleday and Company, Inc., 1976), 57.

Chapter 3
1. Roof and McKinney, *American Mainline Religion*, 22.
2. Ibid., 22.
3. Lyle Schaller, "What Did the Post-Mortem Reveal?" (from *Net Results*, April 1995), 25-28.
4. *The Gallup Poll* (Princeton, N.J.: Princeton Religious Research Center, December 1995).

5. *The Gallup Poll.*

6. Kenneth C. Haugk, *Antagonists in the Church* (Minneapolis: Augsburg Publishing House, 1988), 60-63.

7. Robert N. Bellah, Richard Madsen, Ann Swidler, Steven H. Tipton, *Habits of the Heart* (San Francisco: Harper & Row Publishers, 1985).

8. Hans Selye, *The Stress of Life*, revised edition (New York: McGraw-Hill Book Co., 1956, 1976), 74.

9. Isabel Briggs Myers, *Gifts Differing* (Palo Alto, Calif.: Consulting Psychologists Press, Inc., 1980), 83-116.

10. Barney McLaughlin, *Workshop for a Disciples Assembly*, River Valley District, Paris, Ark., March 1990.

11. Henri Nouwen, *The Wounded Healer* (Garden City, N.Y.: Image Books, 1979), 20.

12. Raymond Bailey, *Thomas Merton on Mysticism* (Garden City, N.Y.: Image Books, 1976), 201.

13. Selye, *The Stress of Life.*

14. H. Beecher Hicks, *Preaching Through the Storm* (Grand Rapids: Zondervan Publishing House, 1987), 17.

15. *Leadership*, Winter 1996.

16. G. Lloyd Rediger, *Clergy Killers* (Inver Grove Heights, Minn.: Logos Productions Inc., 1997), 25.

Chapter 4

1. Lawrence Cada, Raymond Fitz, Gertrude Foley, Thomas Giardino, Carol Lichtenberg, *Shaping the Coming Age of Religious Life* (New York: The Seabury Press, 1979), 53-61.

2. *Shaping the Coming Age*, 53.

3. *Shaping the Coming Age*, 55.

4. *Shaping the Coming Age*, 56.

5. *Shaping the Coming Age*, 57.

6. *Shaping the Coming Age*, 58.

7. *Shaping the Coming Age*, 58.

8. *Shaping the Coming Age*, 59.

9. *Shaping the Coming Age*, 59.

10. Douglas John Hall, *The Steward* (New York: Friendship Press, 1982), 69.

11. Henri Nouwen, *Reaching Out* (Garden City, N.Y.: Doubleday & Co., Inc., 1975), 78.

12. *Reaching Out*, 46.

Chapter 5

1. John W. Gardner, *On Leadership* (New York: The Free Press, 1990), xi.

2. *On Leadership*, 1.

3. John P. Kotter, *Leading Change* (Boston: Harvard Business School Press, 1996), 186.

4. Margaret J. Wheatley, *Leadership and the New Science* (San Francisco: Berrett-Koehler Publishers, Inc., 1992), 133.

5. Kotter, *Leading Change*, 26.

6. Jay A. Conger, *The Charismatic Leader* (San Francisco: Jossey-Bass Publishers, 1989), 17.

7. Conger, *The Charismatic Leader*, 18.

8. Jack R. Gibb, *Trust* (Los Angeles: Guild of Tutors Press, 1978), 13.

9. *Trust*, 14.

10. *Trust*, 14.

11. Roy M. Oswald, Gail D. Hinand, William Chris Hobgood, Barton M. Lloyd, *New Visions for the Long Pastorate* (Washington, D.C.: the Alban Institute, 1983), 42-49.

12. Speed B. Leas, *Should the Pastor Be Fired?* (Washington, D.C.: the Alban Institute, 1980), 5.

13. Conger, *The Charismatic Leader*, 41.

14. David J. Bosch, *Transforming Mission* (Maryknoll, N.Y.: Orbis Books, 1991), 11.

CPSIA information can be obtained
at www.ICGtesting.com
Printed in the USA
LVHW04s1053130518
577027LV00001B

3 4711 00228 9926